Stony the Road
*Chapters in the History
of Hampton Institute*

Stony the Road

Chapters in the History

of Hampton Institute

EDITED BY KEITH L. SCHALL

University Press of Virginia

Charlottesville

THE UNIVERSITY PRESS OF VIRGINIA
Copyright © 1977 by the Rector and Visitors
of the University of Virginia

First published 1977

Library of Congress Cataloging in Publication Data

Main entry under title:

Stony the road.

  Bibliography: p.
  1. Hampton Institute, Hampton, Va.—History.
I. Schall, Keith L., 1943–
LC2851.H32S84   378.755′ 412   76-56224   ISBN 0-8139-0720-9

Printed in the United States of America

To Roy D. Hudson

Contents

Foreword
Roy D. Hudson

RESEARCHING OUR PAST in an effort to better understand the present and chart our future, in the true Bicentennial spirit Hampton Institute is surveying and studying its recently enhanced archival holdings of 800,000 items including 30,000 photographs. The materials in this collection show that Hampton's early history is a story of strong-willed individuals struggling against nearly impossible odds to survive. These materials help explain our nation's history, its growth and development, and the part Hampton Institute has played therein. Hampton Institute, for example, was deeply involved in improving the relationship between the North and the South following the Civil War. Hampton was likewise important in developing educational opportunities for American Indians in the southeastern region of the United States from 1878 to 1923. Moreover, several presidents of our nation were closely associated with Hampton, and their names can be found among the listings of the trustees. This archival collection includes correspondence and other papers of many Americans prominent in the country's history, including Mary McLeod Bethune, George Washington Carver, Frederick Douglass, W. E. B. DuBois, John Hope Franklin, William H. Hastie, James Weldon Johnson, Booker T. Washington, Thurgood Marshall, Franklin Delano Roosevelt, William Howard Taft, and James A. Garfield.

The Archives and Publications Committee, responsible for the present volume, was appointed to support the library staff in the continued development of the Hampton Institute Archives to make the archives useful for the entire campus community. Already this resource is having a profound effect on the campus by providing additional opportunities for faculty writing and research. This subsequently affects our student body, for the student who studies with the professor actively engaged in research and in seeking new information has a decided advantage over the student who studies with the professor largely dependent upon the authority of the written page. Learning to think, to analyze, to question, and to theorize in response to collected facts are primary activities in the educational process. Participating in these expanded research opportunities, several undergraduates at Hampton are currently involved in research studies requiring the use of archival materials. These young people are gaining a new perspective of themselves, their school, and their nation. This thrust has always been important. It is doubly so as Hampton prepares young people to take their places in America during its third century as a nation.

Many significant and interesting episodes in the story of the life of Hampton Institute have remained practically untold for decades. This has been especially true since the demise of the official journal of the college, the *Southern Workman,* in July 1939. With the present volume the Archives and Publications Committee of the college reinstitutes a serious and deep exploration of the college's heritage.

Tempus fugit . . . time flies, and with its flight have come many people and many changes to Hampton Institute, the century-old school along the shores of the Hampton River. These times, recorded in the Hampton Institute Archives, date back to the late nineteenth century, to a period shortly after the Civil War when two teachers and fifteen students held the school's first class beneath the boughs of the Emancipation Oak, a majestic live oak tree with a circumference of ninety-eight yards. This tree, some three-hundred years old, is the oldest living thing on the campus. It "experienced" the dark time of slavery, the Civil War, the Emancipation Proclamation, Reconstruction; it saw the period when four million slaves, 95 percent of whom were illiterate and without resources, were freed in a hostile environment that did not believe in their equality nor accept the thesis that they were educable. It was during this time on April 1, 1868, that the Hampton Normal and Agricultural Institute— now Hampton Institute—stepped into the void, slowly at first but then with ever-increasing effectiveness.

Although Hampton Institute was primarily concerned for the Black freedmen, from its conception it provided education without consideration of race. Its charter, granted by an act of the Virginia General Assembly on June 4, 1870, included the words "without distinction of color." This charter was frequently threatened by a white-dominated legislature in the early days but has remained intact to the present date. The record shows that the first white student enrolled at Hampton just eight years after it opened its doors. This student graduated in 1879. The first American Indian student enrolled in 1878, the first student from China in 1884, the first Turkish student in 1889, and the first Russian girl in 1890. Today the college covers a sprawling campus of 210 acres on the banks of the Hampton River and enrolls a multiethnic student body from thirty-nine states and nineteen foreign countries. Twelve percent of its enrollment is presently non-Black, which continues the provision of the original charter committing the institution to provide an education for all interested persons "without distinction of color."

In this first volume the Archives and Publications Committee shares its research on selected representatives of the Hampton Institute hierarchy: a chairman of the Board of Trustees, a trustee, a principal (later called president) of the institution, a chaplain, a faculty member, students (Black and Red), and a faculty organization. The examples in this vertical profile, representing the primary strata of the institution, have been selected from different times in the life of the school and therefore provide a temporal sense of growth and development. Numbered among these people active in the life of Hampton are William Howard Taft, better known as a president of the United States and later as chief justice of the United States, and James A. Garfield, who was also to become president of our nation. The former served as a trustee (1909–30) of Hampton and chairman (then called president) of the Board of Trustees from 1914 to the time of his death in 1930; the latter served as a trustee from 1870 to 1875.

This volume traces the journey of William H. Sheppard—one of Booker T. Washington's classmates at Hampton—as he walks 260 miles, swims the Kassai River, and travels an additional thirty days by steamboat to a point 1,200 miles into the heart of Africa to become the first Black missionary sent to the Congo. It reiterates the words of President Taft, a trustee of Hampton Institute, as he expresses the belief on June 9, 1912, that even Hampton's founder, General Samuel Chapman Armstrong, did not realize "the tremendous force that this institution which he founded was to exert in the history of this, our country, and in the solution of difficulties, which for years have seemed insoluble." It describes Co-ho-e and Ko-ba, Etah-die-ur, and Tich-ke-met-sa as well as Tsah-dle-tah, who were among the first Indian students to arrive at the campus in 1878. It investigates the ideas of James A. Garfield, trustee of Hampton Institute and soon-to-be president of the United States, as he voices his opinion in a letter to General Armstrong on a subject that later produced such heated debate between Hampton's most famous graduate, Booker T. Washington, and the noted scholar W. E. B. Du Bois: "I would not, if I were in your place, commit myself absolutely to the policy of manual labor schools—as a principle of general application for the reason that hitherto all such experiments have finally failed and for the stronger reason that very much manual labor is inconsistent with a very high degree of mental culture."

This volume examines the life of Professor Jay Saunders Redding, a former Hampton professor (1943–67) and holder of the James Weldon Johnson Distinguished Professorship. It analyzes how the Hampton Institute Camera Club (organized as the Kiquotan Kamera Club on October 21, 1893) illustrated the "soul" of Paul Laurence Dunbar in such poems as "Chris'mus is a-Comin'" and "Two Little Boots." His genius will become all the more visible in "Portraits in Black—Illustrated Poems of Paul Laurence Dunbar."

Lastly, this volume follows Hampton's second president, Hollis Burke Frissell, as he attempts to fill the shoes of the institution's founder. It emphasizes his plight as educator, fund raiser, and president of an educational institution, given the backdrop of the fiscal problems of our colleges and universities today.

Foreword

Young in the annals of Hampton Institute, the Archives and Publications Committee was organized on December 14, 1973. When fully implemented, it will transcend its youth and illuminate the activities of Hampton Institute for the past 108 years, to the credit of all who have joined in making the college and our country what they are.

Preface

LEGENDARY AND HISTORICAL, apocryphal and apotheosized, our heroes have served us well during our brief two hundred years as a nation. But in such repositories as the archives of Hampton Institute lie the records of less renowned people whom conventional history has largely ignored yet whose accomplishments when scrutinized carefully may reveal an epoch, a character, an issue, or an experience more accurately than the lives of our standard heroes.

Thousands of people had crossed that portion of the Delaware River between Pennsylvania and New Jersey just above New Hope; but until General Washington did, the feat was historically meaningless. In the settlement of this continent thousands of Americans moved across the eastern mountain ranges and middle plains; but until Horace Greeley coined his slogan, the fact remained obscure to popular consciousness. Then, under the insight and acuity of thinkers such as Frederick Jackson Turner, the slogan "explained" a half-century or more of American motivation—manifest destiny, the indomitable questing spirit of the pioneers, our will to conquer the physical environment. In this mythical sense we are often conditioned to think that only one man ever crossed the Delaware, and we may find it convenient to believe that only the pioneers represent the strength of the American character. But the individuals whose papers are deposited in Hampton's archives, like the millions who continue to cross the Delaware, have played meaningful parts in our history. Mundane by the measure of national epic, they might have remained unknown, shadowy figures in a society hungry for brilliance, or just now, languidly inclined to soft-edged outlines of nostalgia. Through these people, whose lives touched greater lives and who were often great in their own ways, one can come to a more intimate knowledge of the quiet revolution of Black education generally and of this institution particularly. To bring these figures to light and to analysis is to discover the buried cairns in our history. To read about General Armstrong, Principal Frissell, Paul Laurence Dunbar and his illustrators, William Sheppard, and Saunders Redding is to encounter our heritage, its leaders and plain citizens, and to understand more completely the shape of Black experience too often passed over for the appealing romantic or exciting militant views.

The essays in this volume span nearly the whole of Hampton's history. And recurring in all of them is the theme of change: problem and solution, stimulus and response, pressure and influence, motive and concept. In short, these essays discover Hampton's stony road—the changes in fortune and direction, not of mythic apotheosized heroes and panoramic drama, but real people trying to control their destinies, people who respond and who in turn stimulate, whose purposeful ideas and accomplishments ought to be recognized.

This, the first in a projected series of volumes, draws upon a collection of primary documents—reports, pamphlets, letters, and photographs—rich in ungleaned information. Prominently, for instance, it includes the sixty-seven years of the *Southern Workman,* published at Hampton to give "to its readers the thoughts of Indians, of Negroes, and of Northern and Southern whites" to help them "to understand one another." Now largely organized, the archives contains thousands of items that make the past come alive and document significant portions of black history.

This project owes its genesis to Roy D. Hudson, president of the college, whose foresight brought together the materials scattered across the campus, organizing them for preservation and scrutiny. It owes its momentum to his energy; and what we add to the growing awareness of Black history derives from his initial concept.

This project is indebted to our Archivist, Fritz Malval, himself a walking repository of information, under whose expertise the archives emerged from its inchoate origins. Guidance for the use of this material and the particular impetus for these essays derive from the Archives and Publication

Committee, and credit for the fruition belongs mainly to Nancy B. McGhee and William H. Robinson, whose achievements qualify them for archival study. Funds for preparation of the manuscript were awarded by the Faculty Research Committee. In addition, we owe special thanks to Jason Grant, Head Librarian, who often smoothed our rocky path, to Genevieve Wesley, our meticulous typist, and to Ruben Burrell, our photographer.

KEITH L. SCHALL

Acknowledgments

We are grateful for permission to quote from the following works:

Samuel Chapman Armstrong, letter to Emma Armstrong, April 15, 1878, Armstrong Collection, Williams College, Williamstown, Mass. By permission of Williams College.

Board of Trustees, Hampton Institute, from Minutes. By permission of the Board.

Countee Cullen, from "Yet Do I Marvel," *On These I Stand*. Copyright 1927, 1929, 1935, 1940, 1947, Harper and Row. By permission of the publisher. Originally published in *Color*, 1925.

The Daily Press, Newport News, Va., March 15, 1925, p. 4; July 17, 1925, p. 4; November 28, 1926, pp. 1–2; January 28, 1926, p. 4; February 19, 1926, p. 1. By permission of the publisher.

John Garraty, from *Interpreting American History*. Copyright 1970, The Macmillan Company. By permission of the publisher.

James Weldon Johnson, from *Along This Way*. Copyright 1933 by James Weldon Johnson, copyright © renewed by Grace Nail Johnson. By permission of The Viking Press, Inc.

Rayford Logan, from *Betrayal of the Negro*. By permission of the author.

Jay Saunders Redding, from *An American in India: A Personal Report on the Indian Dilemma and the Nature of Her Conflict*. Copyright 1954 by Saunders Redding. By permission of Bobbs-Merrill Company, Inc.

Jay Saunders Redding, from *On Being Negro in America.* Copyright 1951, by J. Saunders Redding. By permission of Bobbs-Merrill Company, Inc.

Jay Saunders Redding, from *No Day of Triumph.* By permission of the author.

Theodore Clarke Smith, from *The Life of James Abram Garfield.* Copyright 1925, Yale University Press. By permission of the publisher.

Kenneth Stampp, from "Triumph of White Racism," *Blacks in White America since 1865: Issues and Interpretations,* by Robert C. Twombly. Copyright © 1972 by Robert C. Twombly. Reprinted by permission of David McKay Company.

John M. Taylor, from *Garfield of Ohio: The Available Man.* Copyright 1970 by John M. Taylor. By permission of W. W. Norton and Company, Inc.

Darwin Turner, from "Paul Laurence Dunbar: The Poet and the Myths," *CLA Journal,* 18 (Dec. 1974), 155–71. By permission of the publisher.

Hollie I. West, from "Saunders Redding on What It Means to Be Black," The *Washington Post,* January 31, 1971. Sec. K, p. 1, col. 4; p. 4, col. 1. By permission of the publisher.

Stony the Road
*Chapters in the History
of Hampton Institute*

Indian Education at Hampton Institute
William H. Robinson

DURING THE SMALL HOURS of the morning of April 13, 1878, a student guard was patrolling the banks of the Hampton River in front of the Mansion House, residence of Hampton Institute's principal. Looking past the river out to Chesapeake Bay, he discerned the shadowy outline of a large ship steaming slowly toward the school's landing wharf, which jutted out into the water from the edge of the campus. As the ship touched, a man jumped onto the landing platform and tied the rope thrown him to a post, making the steamer *Hampton* fast. Joining the man on the wharf was a man dressed in a U.S. army uniform who immediately began to give orders in a military fashion. Apparently in response to his orders some shadowy figures began to disembark from the ship's lower deck; unlike the military man who gave the orders, those coming off the ship had blankets draped around their shoulders. Very excited and more than a little frightened, the student guard ran to the Mansion House to tell Principal Samuel Chapman Armstrong about the strange human cargo that was unloading on the wharf.[1]

In a letter written to his wife two days after the incident, Armstrong mentioned almost casually the beginning of Indian education at Hampton Institute. He wrote: "Night before last at 2 A.M. I was waked to find that 70 Indians were at the wharf. . . . We waked up everyone . . . put the Indians in two recitation rooms and went to bed again."[2]

But who were these Indians? Where did they come from? How did they happen to come to Hampton Institute? To find the answers to these and similar questions, we must go back to another time, approximately three years before their arrival at Hampton, and to another place, Saint Augustine, Florida.

Early view of Hampton Institute from the Hampton River. *Left,* Young Women's Department with industrial and dining rooms; *left center,* Teachers' Residence; *center,* barn and storehouse; *center foreground,* wharf where the Indians landed in 1878; *right,* Young Men's Department with assembly and recitation rooms

In 1875, at the close of a war with some of the tribes in the Indian territory, seventy-five of their principal chiefs and their boldest followers were selected by the government to be made examples of. They were separated from their friends, some bound hand and foot with manacles and chains, and brought to Saint Augustine. Here the massive gates of Old Fort Marion opened and closed upon them. Capt. R. H. Pratt, the officer in charge of the crew, was a man with a heart and with faith in humanity. The Indian prisoners soon learned that they had a master but also a friend. As soon as new conditions made chains unnecessary, he took them off. But the Indians were confined for three years within the gates of Fort Marion.[3]

During his three years with these Indians, Captain Pratt started to teach them to read. Many ladies of Saint Augustine came to offer their services. These missionary-minded women "came to the Fort and taught the prisoners to read, count, about God, about justice and truth."[4] In addition, one of these teachers sought to get some of her pupils, who now constituted a class, educated at a regular school, and she raised money to send them. After getting them off to school, she had $40 left of the $220 she had solicited, and she so informed Captain Pratt, urging him to send another of the Indian prisoners away to school. Pratt wrote Armstrong requesting him to take an Indian to be educated with a scholarship funded by the $40 surplus. Armstrong wrote him to send the Indian on, although the school would have to see him through financially because there was not enough money in the scholarship.[5]

It appears that Armstrong expected one Indian instead of the seventy who actually arrived. Not all were to stay at Hampton, however. Three months after their arrival, Armstrong informed the school's Board of Trustees of the new educational adventure: "Curiously, without effort on our part or expense to the school, there are seventeen Indian youth."[6] The number that actually remained at Hampton was fifteen; later two others who had left returned. Thus the first Indians who came to Hampton Institute were not students in search of education but prisoners of war who really did not know where they were going or why.

Hampton could not develop a meaningful educational program for only seventeen Indians. However, with an eye to the pioneering possibilities in American education, Armstrong took steps to build up the Indian enrollment at the school. He requested and got permission of General William Tecumseh Sherman and the secretary of the interior to have fifty Indians sent to Hampton Institute. Captain Pratt was instructed to secure twenty-five females and twenty-five males from the upper Missouri. But, as it was later reported, "on the 5th day of November 1878, forty-nine Indian youth, nine of them girls, were brought here from ... agencies in Dakota Territory, selected by Captain R. H. Pratt of the U.S. Army, under instructions from the department of Indian Affairs at Washington."[7]

To report without elaboration that Captain Pratt brought forty-nine Indians to Hampton Institute might give two impressions—both wrong. The manner in which the small first groups were brought to Hampton Institute foreshadowed the procedure that would be followed for years to come. Pratt did not again bring prisoners of war as was the case with the first group but literally beat the bushes to round up the second

Capt. R. H. Pratt, who brought the first group of Indians to Hampton Institute in 1878

group.[8] The nature of his involvement is best described in his
own words in a letter written to General Armstrong from Sioux
City, Iowa, October 10, 1878:

I telegraphed a question to you from Fort Thompson on the 29th of
September to which I have received no response. I now ask you to

telegraph me on the receipt of this, directing to Bismark, whether you think we are not able to carry, through private charity, twenty to thirty—over and above the fifty Commissioner Hayt will pay for. I think we can. . . . I should start from [Fort] Berthold with fifteen to twenty, then if other agencies fail (which I very much apprehend, because there is so much disturbance along the river just now) I would come out about even. . . . I do not want to risk my health, further, in a visit to the Indian territory now. . . . I have lived hard and my old enemy hurts me. . . . There should have been five hundred Indians from here, instead of fifty, to be educated. . . . I hope to be back in three weeks. There will be scurrility on the frontier about this effort.[9]

Pratt's journeys to recruit Indian students for the Hampton school were obviously not only difficult but dangerous as well. He wrote of having "a hard time," of riding "659 miles in wagons and stages in thirteen days travel," and of the hostility of many of the Indian chiefs toward the attempts to recruit young Indians to attend a boarding school. Pratt signaled the end of this particular search with a brief note from Yankton, Dakota Territory, on October 31, to Armstrong: "You have forty boys and nine girls; leave in the morning."[10]

Now, nearly one hundred years later, as they have vanished from many places that were their native habitat, Indians have also vanished from Hampton Institute, leaving some reminders that they were here.

Near the center of the campus is a recently refurbished building bearing the name Wigwam. Just outside the main entrance to the campus, but on college-owned land, is a dormitory called by the Indian name Winona. The one-way, no-exit entrance to the campus is Indian Road. Indian relics and artifacts decorate the walls of the college museum, and pictorial displays of Indian life and customs frequently adorn the library's exhibit cases. Along the side of a usually deserted pathway near the lower eastern side of the campus not far from the water's edge is the college's cemetery, a portion of which deserves recognition as a miniature Indian burying ground containing headstones on which are carved the names of those who have long since joined their ancestors.

The few remaining signs, all but invisible today, leave little to remind one that Indians were here. But the native Americans did come to Hampton Institute to be civilized and to learn "the white man's road." Among the first to arrive were Indian braves who bore such musical names as Co-ho-e and Ko-ba. Etah-die-ur and Tich-ke-met-sa came also. Tsah-dle-tah was here too.[11]

Later the chiefs came—tall in stature, noble in bearing, and stoic in expression, wearing the colorful leather and feathered trappings of the hunt and the warpath, the chiefs of many tribes. Although too old to learn the "white man's road" themselves, they nevertheless came to see at firsthand what an off-reservation boarding school could do to civilize the heirs-apparent to the great legacy of the native American. The chiefs came and liked what they saw; so when they departed, they gave their blessings to a scheme which, if successful, would someday sound the death knell of a noble tradition. These chiefs, whose names were spoken with awe and reverence across the Great Plains and in Indian territories throughout the nation, included Black Horse, a Comanche chief, whose statement made to an assembly of students and teachers had to be translated because he spoke no English. He referred to the federal government as "Washington," and his remarks were translated into these words by Captain Pratt: "A long time ago Washington talked to me. I was growing up from a little boy; Washington kept talking to me. Washington gave me a road. . . . I was steady on it sometimes, but I kept tumbling off. Just now I am fixed upon it. . . . Whatever road Washington gives to me now, I am going to pick it up, and carry it out with me to Indian territory. . . . I have looked all around and seen what white man can do, and I have found the white man is way ahead of everybody I know anything about."[12] In the two years he had spent under Captain Pratt's charge as a prisoner of war at Fort Marion, the chief had learned his lessons well. Whether by indoctrination, intimidation, or education, the old Indian had embraced the "white man's road."

Lone Wolf, who had tried two years before to escape from the Fort Marion prison, seems also to have been converted to the "white man's road." In Captain Pratt's translation: "Tonight I have a little talk for the white people. A long time ago, all these young men and old men did not understand the white man. God has given him, and all Indians, a road. It is the very same road the white people have. It is God's road for all men. . . . The same things are for the red man as for the white man."[13] Evidently Chief Lone Wolf had gotten religion—the white man's religion. He felt that he had learned the "white man's road." Only a few came at first, but later they were to come in larger numbers so that during the forty-five years of Hampton's Indian program 1,388 of them would pass this way.

Hampton's experiment in Indian education was highly controversial. Armstrong was often called on to explain and frequently to defend nearly every development that took place in the program. In fact, no sooner did it become known that the first group of Indians had arrived at the school than a great debate was joined, one that would last for more than thirty years.

At Hampton and throughout the nation, many issues concerning the "Indian problem" were raised. First among these problems relevant to Hampton Institute was whether the Indians could be educated. Even if they could be, one argument asked, would they remain so or would they "return to the blanket" once they left the school and resumed tribal life? Among those who emerged as chief critics of the Hampton program were individuals who questioned the propriety of having Indians attend school with Blacks, with the onus being placed on the latter. Should the culture of Indians be emphasized in their education, or should they be anglicized? Should Indians be Christianized? Would the Indians adapt to the demands of a laboring society? These were some of the many issues and questions that were raised in the halls of Congress, in the Bureau of Indian Affairs, and across the nation. All these and many other issues and questions regarding the Indians were addressed at Hampton Institute. In a real sense the school evolved as a microcosm of Indian affairs.

The manner in which the nation, and particularly the government, dealt with problems involving the Indian was greatly influenced by the procedures followed at Hampton. Through letters, speeches, and published articles, Armstrong personally debated with the secretary of the interior and the

commissioner of Indian affairs on most of the crucial issues
involving the welfare of the Indians. He also took pains to react
to nearly every position taken by anyone anywhere on every
matter of importance to the Indians. Often taking exception to
those in authority, Armstrong made clear his views concerning
how problems involving the Indians should be handled at the
school and in the nation.

A mirror of Indian affairs at the national level, Hampton Institute set the example for Indian education that was to be
followed by all off-reservation schools in the country. An
official report prepared under the direction of Walton C. John
of the staff of the U.S. Bureau of Education with an introduction by William Howard Taft, chief justice of the United States,
reaffirmed Hampton's influence on Indian education: "So
marked was the success of the experiment at Hampton Institute that a public sentiment in favor of Indian education was
created. From this small beginning has grown the present
system of Government Indian education."[14] Captain Pratt, the
army officer who brought the first contingent of Indian
students to Hampton, offered this comment: "Without the
open door at Hampton, none of the advanced conditions in Indian school affairs to-day would have become established. It
would be difficult to locate the critical period in the development of the movement, but certainly Hampton and Armstrong
. . . can claim one of the foremost emergency positions."[15]

The initial question was whether the Indian could be "civilized." This question was as philosophically and morally profound as any that could be asked about a people or race. It was
in essence the primary question, however answered. If the
answer was yes, the subsequent questions about how, where,
and when would have to be answered. If the answer was no, the
prospect would be worse; such an answer would lead to elimination of the Indians.

Despite the absence of precedent and the possible ramifica-
tions of the answer, Armstrong took the firm and unequivocal
stand that most certainly the Indian could be civilized. This
stance harmonized perfectly with his belief that providence
had called him to help uplift the Black race. With the same
spirit he could uplift another downtrodden people.

Armstrong apparently understood all that civilizing the Indians implied. It meant changing them culturally into Eu-
ropeans, eradicating their traditional ways of life that allowed
them to be free spirits living close to nature, and replacing that
mode of existence with an alien one based on binding
constraints in a controlled social order. Specifically, it meant
throwing off buckskins and blanket and drawing on trousers,
shirt, and tie. It meant abandoning the tepee and taking shelter
in a house. It meant giving up their own languages and learning to speak English. It also meant abrogating tribal relations
and accepting the ideal of individuality. Braves would have to
abandon the hunt and warpath and pursue a life of gainful
labor. This well may have been their greatest loss because it
meant that the noble hunters and warriors would be reduced to
the ignominy of earning their livelihood through time-
measured labor. The status of Indian women would also un-
dergo many drastic changes. From drudges, almost slavelike,
the one-time squaws would now be mothers and homemakers
by white men's standards.

Those who thought the Indians could in fact be civilized also
thought that they would have to worship the white man's God
instead of their own Great Spirit: to them, to civilize meant to
Christianize. Christianity was the primary source of the Red
men's mortal as well as immortal salvation. Ironically, even the
avowed friends of the Indians seemed to have ignored the obvious fact that they were profoundly religious although they
were not followers after Christ. Evidently religious freedom did
not extend to those who, although they were the true natives,
were not citizens but strangers in their own land.

Those who doubted that the Indians could be civilized were
probably in the majority, as Armstrong noted: "Some experienced teachers and army officers prophesy a relapse of educated Indians on their return to their homes, from opposition,
from ridicule, and shock at the old life and from the force of
circumstances."[16] But by the very act of accepting Indians as
students in the school, Armstrong left no doubt concerning his
convictions. Later he was to answer a related question: "If the
Indian is civilized, will he remain civilized or will he return to
the 'blanket'?" In his first annual report to the commissioner of

Indian affairs made in 1882, Armstrong observed that the civilizing process had been successful and the "return to the blanket" a most unlikely prospect. In his report on a follow-up study of the return of twenty-five male and five female Sioux youths to their homes in Dakota, he gave, among other equally successful stories, the following accounts:

Rev. Jno. P. Williamson, a veteran missionary, writes of the six who returned to the Yankton Agency—"So far they have all run well. . . . They attend church regularly; they are recognized as leading spirits among the Christian youth; their appearance is always creditable. Not one white boy in sixteen could do his work or teach as well as David Simmons. . . .

Major Parkhurst, agent at Lower Brule, reports . . . [on] the five young men returned to this agency: "All the returned boys from Hampton have now come in and are at work, doing much better."[17]

Armstrong also informed the commissioner that "three boys and one girl are at Crow Creek Agency, the latter keeping her father's store and accounts, and doing well at last reports. The two shop boys, carpenters, are reported as 'doing all that could be expected,' and the teacher as 'doing splendidly.' They are exerting a good influence on the Indians around them." Continuing, Armstrong reported that "five returned boys are at Cheyenne River; one is assistant teacher, the rest are mechanics, blacksmiths, and carpenters, making an excellent record; like the others in government shops, at moderate wages, and wholly supporting themselves. All or nearly all at the various agencies live away from the tents or camps in decent rooms at the headquarters." He further reported that "two boys and one girl are at Standing Rock Agency. Major McLaughlin, in charge, writes: 'Both the young men are doing well.' A lady missionary reports that 'they are quiet, conscientious workers, and have the respect of every one.' The girl is working in a missionary's family giving excellent satisfaction."[18]

These are but random samples of the evidence Armstrong early presented to the commissioner of Indian affairs and to the nation to prove that native Indians could be civilized and would remain civilized. During the decade 1882–92 Armstrong would report follow-up surveys of nearly every In-

dian who came to Hampton Institute. The proof that these Indians became civilized was incontrovertible, and a rough estimate is that more than four-fifths of them successfully adopted
the "white man's road."

Armstrong's means of civilizing the Indians was an education
that stressed basic skills and industrial and agricultural training. Consensus of those who favored educating the Indians was
that two major objectives should be sought: to help the Indians
regain their self-respect and to make them self-supporting.
Armstrong's conviction was that the educational plan the school
had been providing for Black men for a decade would enable
the Red men to realize these two objectives. He saw similarities
in the conditions of the two races. Armstrong reasoned well
through implication; he sought to restore self-respect within
the Red men as in Black men. Black men had lost self-respect in
slavery, Red men through subjugation on reservations. Black
men had their self-respect taken from them when they were
forced to slave for white masters; Red men lost their self-
respect as a result of being cut off from the chase and the hunt.
Certainly a contributing factor was the loss of their leaders.
Black men lost their leaders in mid-passage; Red men in wars
with the white man through death or capture.

The Hampton education plan had two major components.
The practical aspect, aimed mainly at self-support, can be
described rather simply and directly. In addition to learning
how to read, speak, and write English and to use numbers cor-
rectly, the Indians were taught agriculture and trades, including carpentry, shoemaking, butchering, tinsmithing, black-
smithing, printing, wheelwrighting, harnessmaking, and basic
engineering. Self-respect cannot, of course, be directly taught
but comes indirectly from mastering various skills. Almost
every situation involving the development of skills in farming
and in trades was utilized to help the Indian students develop
character, an important aspect of self-respect.

Education to develop self-respect as members of the white
man's culture was a very complicated matter for the Indians. It
involved the acquisition of new values, new ideas, and new life-
styles. The Indians would have to develop new ways of looking
at the world and their fellowmen and especially new and dif-

ferent views of themselves. Obviously, the problem here was getting them to view themselves as worthy human beings in an alien setting rather than to internalize the white man's unfavorable view of them.

Despite the enormity of the problems involved, Armstrong felt confident that the Hampton plan would succeed. Within a month after the first group of Indians arrived at Hampton, Armstrong said, "I think this school can indicate one way in which the Indian may be educated to his own advantage, and to the country."[19]

The plan for educating the Indian students at Hampton reflects the laborious process of basic learning, a process further complicated and slowed by their resentment of the white man's lessons. After approximately four years of experimentation, the curriculum of the Indian education program was fairly well set. In his 1882 *Annual Report* to the commissioner of Indian affairs, Armstrong described the instructional program in detail:

During the school year, there have been in the regular classes of the normal school, fifteen Indians (senior class—3, middle class—1, junior class—11), the remainder being separated into six divisions according to their ability and progress in English. It is evident that as the majority of these have little or no knowledge of the language the teaching must be for a long time wholly oral. The course which has been developed by the necessities and circumstances of the case I can best briefly describe by quoting from the report of Miss H. W. Ludlow, teacher of English:

"FIRST YEAR. 1. *Teaching by objects.* Names of things: Boy, book. Description of qualities: Tall boy, red book. Pronouns: You and I, it, etc. Actions performed, asserted, commanded: I walk, she walked, walk. . . . Classes of objects are naturally taught together to aid the memory by association, and the object itself is used whenever possible. Toys and pictures representing them are used in other cases. . . .

"2. All sorts of talking games have been devised. . . .

"3. Short dialogues, memorized and repeated daily. . . .

"SECOND YEAR. Cheap chromo-lithographs, large enough for all to see, are now employed to develop the power of expression. Perhaps the teacher begins 'I see a horse.' Someone is sure to take it up, and soon all are vying with each other to tell what they see in the picture books before them. . . . Letter writing is used to some extent,

Indians learning to farm

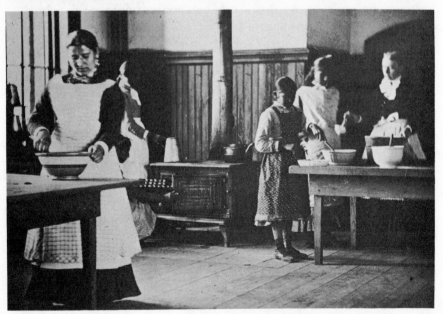

Indian girls learning to cook

the letters being written on the board by the teacher, the sentences given orally by the pupils. . . .

"FOURTH YEAR. In this year for the first time, a book is placed in the hands of the talking class. . . . In geography our Indians are reported as being thoroughly at home. It has a flavor of the earth, and brings before them vividly the life and surroundings which are dear to them. . . . Instruction in American history is, as may be imagined, somewhat difficult, and is further complicated for the teacher by her realization that 'there is some doubt as to how the graphic descriptions of the aborigines, with scalping knife and tomahawk, will strike their descendants and how they will relish the comments of the historian, sometimes by no means flattering. . . .' In their sewing and cooking classes . . . the girls have had thorough and efficient instruction. . . . The girls are all, so far as practicable, trained in housework, and the fact that they do not take to it naturally and can with difficulty be made to see the importance of it is only the logical result of their previous habits of life."[20]

The Indians appeared to have progressed more rapidly in their acquisition of skills in the trades and in agriculture than they did in academic work. The principal's report mentions a dozen boys doing sophisticated carpentry work and others working in the paint shop. Three were making harnesses and ten were making shoes—all for the Interior Department. Thirty-five were working at Heminway Farm.[21]

The foregoing is typical of the activities provided by Hampton for the Indian students during their early days at the school. Although the level of the academic program was raised as the students entered with some skill in the use of English acquired in mission schools, the basic pattern remained essentially the same during the subsequent years. On the other hand, an innovative feature of the instructional program deserves special mention, namely, the arrangement of the curriculum into several divisions, an organizational procedure which antedated the nongraded approach found in progressive schools today.

The Indians came to the school with such varied levels of preparation that it was impossible to employ the usual placement by grades or the equivalent in such classifications as freshmen, sophomores, juniors, and seniors. It was not even practical to classify Indian students as first year, second year, and third year although the expected stay at the school was three years. The level of readiness to learn ranged all the way from students who could not write in their own dialect to those who had several years of mission school education.

To cope with the situation, the school established divisions representing seven levels of academic competency. This arrangement enabled each student to start at the level at which he was able to perform and to move at his own pace as he improved academically. The students started at different levels when they entered the school: some starting at the lowest level—the first division—and others at more advanced levels. Each student would complete the requirements for as many levels as he could during his stay at the school. Occasionally the students who had spent several years at a mission school would start in the upper divisions and would enter the normal school before leaving, sometimes completing the normal course for the teacher.[22]

The practical nature of the training in the trades and agriculture is evident. Neither was busywork. The Indians learned trades by working at them, making products that were sold. Hampton also provided a special kind of learning-by-doing in the agricultural part of the practical program. It required the boys who remained at the school during the summer months to fulfill all the duties of regular farmers at Shellbanks, a large tract of rich farmland. Indians learned to farm by farming.

Many of those who did not stay at school during the summer months participated in a program called "outing." Starting in 1879, this project placed Indian boys and girls in homes with families in the East and North. The boys learned farming and the girls learned at firsthand skills involved in housekeeping. In addition, they were introduced to family and farm life as well as to the white man's morals and manners.

Typical of the descriptions of summer outing experiences Armstrong included in his reports is the following: "Places for the summer in Berkshire Co., Mass., have been secured for twenty-five Indian boys and girls, each one in a separate home, to work out living expenses under the care of kind and excellent people, with whom they will learn the language rapidly and get a three and a half month's drill in practical living and working as valuable, I think, as any school experience."[23]

In an article entitled "Industrial Training for Indian Children," Estelle Reel summed up the philosophy underlying the outing experience:

This [program] gives the pupil a chance to see the application to home life of the methods and principles in which he is being trained; thus he is led to feel that these principles lie at the foundation of human prosperity and constitute the difference between the prosperous and happy communities of the states, and the hard, ignorant, hand-to-mouth conditions of the tribe. Through this system the pupil is enabled to take a broader view of the great purposes of life; and whether he desires to remain in the midst of civilization and become a part of it, or to return and take up land in severalty; we feel that he has been taught "how to live" and that he may safely go forth to work out his own destiny like the rest of mankind.[24]

According to Armstrong in 1882, the program was a moral and educational success: "For the summer vacation 19 boys and 8 girls have been sent to Berkshire, Mass., under the charge of Hon. Marshall Bidwell of Monteray, Mass., who has found homes for them among the country farmers, where they get a discipline and experience which the experiment of last summer has shown to be of great value."[25]

The first work-study program in American education might have had its beginning at Hampton Institute. Hampton sent Indian students on the outing projects not only for the summer but, as interns, for an entire year at a time. In his 1883 *Annual Report* Armstrong informed the Board of Trustees of a program that went beyond summer outing: "Arrangements have been made to send North twenty-five of our [Indian] youth who have, in response to a suggestion, applied to be sent for a year to farmers of Berkshire, Mass."[26]

The Indians were trained in trades and agriculture so that they could become self-supporting. Armstrong and his co-workers probably did not use the term *self-respect* per se, but in all likelihood they had this concept firmly fixed in their minds. Philosophically, it meant helping the Indians regain in white culture what white men had taken away from them—their status as human beings. Certainly the Indians had great self-respect before the white man came. But the social milieu in which this self-respect was attained and maintained was radically altered by a different set of values introduced into the Indians' cultural system. White culture so completely reversed the Indian's self-image that the crucial question became whether Indians could regain their self-respect as Indians or whether they had to become white men culturally to survive as fulfilled human beings.

Present-day anthropologists term these two conflicting points of view *cultural relativism* and *cultural absolutism*. Cultural absolutism would bring about a complete change in the Indians' ideals, values, morals, customs, religion, and outlook on life. On the other hand, cultural relativism would result in the Indians' preserving some of the basic elements of their culture while becoming acclimated to the white man's culture in ways necessary to their survival and successful functioning among whites. Evidently Armstrong steered a course somewhere between the extremes of these two positions, inclining toward cultural absolutism in some matters and cultural relativism in others. For example, he felt that the Indians should become citizens and exercise all the rights and privileges pertaining thereto but should at the same time preserve certain aspects of Indian culture, particularly their art and literature. Armstrong tried to help the Indians regain their self-respect by encouraging them to adopt the "white man's road." It is clear from many of his utterances on Christianity and the Indians that Armstrong believed they could gain their self-respect and the respect of white men only by becoming Christians.[27] All avowed friends of the Indians saw Christianity as the way to change them from savages of less than human stature to self-respecting and respected human beings.[28]

Armstrong saw labor as a moral force and work as a means of salvation second only to Christianity as the way to restore their self-respect. Dignified, efficacious work and well-developed work habits could restore their morality, the first step in acquiring a new sense of personal worth.[29]

Many problems continued to plague the administration, teachers, and workers at Hampton for the duration of the Indian program at the school. One was the Indians' health; another was their attendance at a school where Blacks were also being educated. Both problems emerged when the first group of Indian prisoners was brought to the school in 1878. Armstrong and his successors in the principalship made noteworthy progress with respect to the Indians' health problems, but a satisfactory solution to the second problem eluded them. The latter, which became known as the "race problem," not only persisted to the end of the program but was directly responsible for the withdrawal of federal support of the program in 1912.

Armstrong was deeply concerned about the Indians' susceptibility to tuberculosis, a gravely serious condition, he thought, inherent in their way of life. "It is well understood that the health question is a serious one in all efforts for the civilization of a race, so serious that it has been made the ground of argument against all attempts at Indian civilization."[30] Thus Armstrong commented in his report for the first full year that Indians were at the school. In the same report he added:

Since the warm weather there is a general improvement in the health of our Indian pupils, though at least one cannot live much longer. Indian girls lead a life of steady work, free from fashion, and hence have strong, well-formed bodies, of natural shape. Their average health is notably better than that of the young men. . . . The boys bred to idleness, acting only in a spasmodic way, have far less vigor and, from their habits of lying around, suffer from exposure of all kinds, especially from the dampness of the ground. Some mortality among these youth may be expected, and should not be charged against the effort to educate them.[31]

An account of the status of the Indian students' health as reported to him by the person in charge of the program was included in Armstrong's 1881 *Annual Report:* "Their health has proved the most serious question in the problem; 15 students, 30 percent of the 49 brought by Capt. Pratt have broken down in health during the three years; 10 of these (20 percent of the whole number brought) have died, either at school or after their return to their homes. It is fair to say that this does not seem to be due so much to the change to civilized life, as to inherited weakness and diseased constitutions and to an utter disregard to all the laws of health."[32]

In his *Annual Report* for 1883, Armstrong noted some improvement in the general health of the Indians and made this encouraging statement: "The health question, which threatened to be an obstacle, if not a fatal barrier to Indian education at the East, has been to a degree settled. It is proved we think, that constant care, regular life, and instruction in the laws of health, improve the physical condition of the Indian in spite of the change of climate and new mode of life to which he is subjected."[33]

In the principal's report of 1884, the shortest and by far the best mention of the health of the Indian students to date was made: "With an exception of an epidemic of mumps, the health of the [Indian] school, during the greater part of the year, has been very good." The situation continued to improve and in his 1886 *Annual Report* Armstrong was able to record: "This year's health record of our Indians has been most gratifying." In subsequent reports little or no reference was made to the health of the Indian students. It appears that the problem had been brought under control, and in 1892 the school physician reported that "there had been no deaths during the term."[34]

Almost at the very beginning of the Indian education program at Hampton, Armstrong and his workers had to deal with problems caused by racism. Incident to the recruiting activities involved in bringing the second group of Indian students to the school in 1879, Armstrong reported that "the girls from this [Cheyenne River] agency were at the last moment led to abandon their intention through prejudice against Hampton Institute as a colored institution, existing in the minds of educators at the Agency, which the officer who had undertaken the task of getting them found impossible to overcome in the short time at his disposal. I found this prejudice more or less at the several other agencies . . . and with like effect on the girls."[35]

Despite this incident and the many questions that were raised about educating Blacks and Indians together, Armstrong was not dismayed: "I was asked is there going to be a war of two races here? Shall we have trouble between these two races brought together here for the first time? I answer NO! God has intended good in this or why has He put into the hearts of so

many people to come forward with their money? He has smiled
upon this undertaking. There will be no trouble, they will all be
friends."[36]

Year after year Armstrong sought to assure the commissioner of Indian affairs that all was well with respect to the
coeducation of the races at the school: "The mingling of the
black and red races in the past seven years has worked well. . . .
Each race has learned much from and been helpful to the
other. There is no friction and no nonsense about race superiority. That this is a school for the uncivilized of any race is
illustrated by the fact that several youths of various na-
tionalities, especially Asiatics who have drifted to this country,
have applied for admission during the past year."[37]

Armstrong consistently took an optimistic view with regard
to the coeducation of the two races and saw the situation as
mutually beneficial: "There is no difficulty from prejudice. The
Negro is a help to the Indian as an example, by his habit of
study and of labor, of obedience of behavior, of general decency, and by his knowledge of English. The latter is here in an
atmosphere of industry, good conduct, and in our language
which does much for his progress."[38] Cora M. Folsom, one of
the teachers who spent most of her time working with the Indians, noted that "many of the teachers feared trouble and
some of the trustees had very serious misgivings over so radical
an innovation, but the General's enthusiasm carried the day."[39]

Criticism of the coeducation of the races at Hampton came
from a wide variety of sources. The *Southern Workman* replied
to an article that had appeared in the New York *Herald* which
stated that people from the city of Hampton as well as other
Virginians opposed the education of the two races together.
But Armstrong held fast to his position: "Sending them [In-
dians] to a Negro school is like putting raw recruits into an old
regiment. The examples, ideas, language, etc., at Hampton are
a constant and powerful educating influence; an atmosphere
which they [Indians] breathe."[40] "There is no contempt for the
negro. A colored non-commissioned officer has more influence
over a Dakota Indian than has a Cheyenne of like position."[41]

Four years after the first Indians entered the school
Armstrong reported that the problems incident to the presence

of the two races at the school were being satisfactorily solved. "The . . . vexed question of the mingling of the races, seems to have satisfactorily settled itself with little or no interference on the part of our officers. I am convinced that there is nothing better for a wild Indian boy, fresh from the plains, than to room for six months with a good colored student, for such companionship does much, in a quiet way, for his habits, manners, and morals."[42]

But despite Armstrong's protestations to the contrary, the problems of race relations at the school did not disappear. His successor, Hollis Burke Frissell, who served as principal from 1893 to 1917, was to report that harmony existed between the races. It appears that he, like Armstrong, was correct in contending that there was a minimum of conflict between the Red men and the Black. The apprehensions that came from outside the college walls were centered on the association between the two races, not on the conflict between them. Here again is another example to show that Hampton Institute was in fact a microcosm of national Indian affairs. In the nation generally there was very strong sentiment against the two races associating with each other, and particularly there was stern opposition to intermarriage. Those who were in authority in the management of Indian affairs for the government were so afraid that intermarriage would take place that Frissell felt constrained to assure them that none had occurred when, in fact, there were reports that such had taken place.[43]

The charge that the school institutionalized racism seems to have been largely unfounded. It was logical to have some racial segregation as well as some integration in the management of the program of education for the two races. In her definitive study of the Indian education program at Hampton, Helen W. Ludlow explains the presence of dormitories for Indian students where they lived separately from the Black students. Winona Lodge for Indian girls and Wigwam for Indian boys were erected to fulfill, in part, an agreement the school had with the federal government. She wrote of "the conflict of races":

As the question of bringing Indians and Negroes together for education at Hampton has always been a subject of interested inquiry and

A young warrior and his bride, both Hampton students

sometimes of adverse prophecy and criticism, it is well to bring it to the front.

As it has been said, as far as the St. Augustine Indians were concerned . . . the question seemed disposed of at once by the hearty cheerfulness with which they all fell into line with their Negro comrades. . . . More or less prejudice of color has been shown occasionally, by some from Indian territory, where Indians held slaves, and by some others.

The vast preponderance of experience has been one of harmony and mutual helpfulness. The first party of Dakotas that came had not been here a month when they petitioned to have colored roommates in order to get on faster in English and civilized customs. The growth of numbers and the necessity of special instruction and management have made this no longer possible, and have tended in a degree to separation. But it is the universal testimony of all here who have the management of both together, that association with his colored school mates, in the classroom, or workshops, on the farm, in the battalion, and such social life as they share, is in many ways of direct benefit to the Indian.[44]

There were separate facilities and other distinctions made along racial lines, but these seem to have been made in response to pressure brought upon the school by outside forces, particularly by government agencies. Even the local community appeared apprehensive, and the editor of the *Southern Workman* responded almost apologetically to an article that appeared in the New York *Herald* which claimed that the people of Virginia were dismayed over the coeducation of the races at the Hampton school: "We [at Hampton] believe that Virginians will not object to teaching the Indians THOSE things that are vital to their well-being, even if the work shall be done in a Negro institute especially since it alone has the facilities for doing such work."[45] In 1897 Frissell called attention to increased integration of the races at the school: "Our Indian school has been less distinct from the rest of the institution and with most excellent results. The Indian boys and girls have been able to take and hold their places by the side of the colored students in the school rooms and shops."[46] Actually there were several incidents of discrimination both within the school itself and in the community. One was the arrangement by which an Indian basketball team played against local white teams, an activity denied to the Black basketball players. There was also an all-Indian battalion. The Indians were allowed to worship at the local churches but the Black students were excluded from these holy places of worship. While traveling with the Negro Quartet for fund-raising purposes, the Indians were permitted to stay in hotels where Blacks were not allowed. Clearly the ambivalent status of the two races, the result of public opinion, was not successfully resisted within the school.

The overall evidence seems to show that the school would have worked out any problems caused by the presence of the two races together at the school. Such was not to be the case, for as badly treated by the white man as were the Indians, Black men were still even more despised. Under community pressure Frissell felt called to explain:

The presence in the school life of Indians, while it gives rise to some complications and makes separate quarters and tables necessary, has given opportunity for the study of the race problems in a broader way than would otherwise have been possible . . . while each race has its own social life, so far as is known, no interracial marriage has ever resulted from the bringing together of these races at Hampton, and an important demonstration has been made of the possibilities of harmonious cooperation between them.[47]

Frissell's assurances were evidently not enough. Responding to public opposition to the coeducation of the Black and the Red races at Hampton, in 1912 Congress voted to end the appropriations to the school for the support of Indian education. The *Southern Workman* reported the circumstance editorially: "Hampton Institute loses, this year, the appropriation by the Government of its Indian students. . . . It may be of interest to note that the appropriation as included in the Indian appropriation Bill as passed by the Senate, but was omitted in the House Bill and was cut out in conference. . . . One of the reasons, perhaps the chief reason, given for the cutting off of this appropriation is the undesirability of mingling Indian and Negro students in the same school."[48]

His preoccupation with the controversy involving the coeducation of the two races did not deter Armstrong from addressing yet another controversial issue. At a time when the nation was primarily interested in educating its boys, Armstrong took a very strong and consistent position for the education of girls. Just as he had called the education of Negro girls necessary to the salvation of the race, so did he give equal priority to the education of Indian girls. He did not have the opportunity to express his views on the sex distribution of the first group of Indians but had this to say about the second group to come to the school: "A few weeks after the arrival of the ex-prisoners of war, I called on . . . the Secretary of the Interior, to suggest that the so far very encouraging experience in Indian civilization be tried more fully by bringing some younger material, girls especially. I urged that there is no civilization without educated women."[49] He stressed the importance of educating the Indian women: "In getting more Indians, the point made at the last annual meeting was the need of girls to offset the young men, for relapse was inevitable should they return home to mate themselves with savages."[50]

Armstrong never ceased in his attempt to enroll more Indian girls in the school, but he was never able to attract as many as he wanted. His first disappointment in this matter came when he requested Captain Pratt to recruit fifty Indian students for the 1879 school year. Pratt was able to bring forty-nine students to the campus of whom only nine were girls. Although Indian girls did come in increasingly large numbers, Armstrong was never able to achieve the desired fifty-fifty ratio of boys to girls. He took the position that the Indian race would not rise much higher than the level of their women, who were so influential in the home. One of the women teachers reportedly said: "The General's [Armstrong's] slogan in his winter campaign has been: 'The condition of women is the test of progress. The family is the unit of Christian civilization. Girls make the mothers. Mothers make the home.' "[51]

As part of his pioneering work in the education of Indians, Armstrong was also ahead of his time in providing education for married couples and their children. In his report to the commissioner of Indian affairs in 1883, Armstrong wrote:

A feature of this year's work has been the taking of young married people as students in the school. Three such couples have been received—Two from the Omaha tribe and one from the Sioux tribe.

The Sioux and one of the Omaha each brought with them a little pa-
poose about a year old. The parents attend school half a day and work
the other half with the other scholars. We have attempted at
Hampton nothing more hopeful than this in training Indians. The
husband and wife advance together with common interests. A home
will be established on their return to the reservation, and their future
will be comparatively secure.[52]

Armstrong called attention to the salutary effect this arrangement had on the Indian mother and father.

It is interesting to note, as side issues in this experiment, the increase
of courtesy in the brave and his wife and the growing care of the
mother for her child, and the effort she makes to keep her husband's
possessions, her room, and her babe, and last of all herself, clean and
tidy. It is touching, too, to watch the increasing tenderness of the
father to his child. At first the father evidently regarded tending the
little bit of humanity with scorn, and the woman carried the heavy
baby, while the man walked unburdened beside her. But the father
grows to take great pride in his boy, and often relieves the mother
now of part of the burden. He is never urged to this course, but is
probably aware that it gives great satisfaction.[53]

In setting forth the purpose of the school at the time of its
founding, Armstrong had written: "The thing to do was clear:
to train selected Negro youths who should go out and teach and
lead the people, first by example, by getting land and homes . . .
[to train them] to build up an industrial system for the sake not
only of self-support and intelligent labor, but also for the sake
of character."[54] Since he saw their needs to be basically similar
to those of Blacks, Armstrong sought to train the Indian
students so that they could return to their people and work for
their welfare. In a paper read to the National Educational
Association in 1884, he stated his position with regard to the
education of Indians: "My own view is that Indians at our
Eastern schools who, to begin with, have a strong home and
filial feeling, and would seldom consent to settle permanently
among strangers, should be taught that they have a duty to
their people; that education is more than preparation for their
own support and decent living, but that they have a great work
. . . and expect to return to teach by precept and example a
more excellent way."[55]

Consistent with the Hampton idea was the concept that the Indian students should be educated not merely for their benefit but also for the contribution they would make to the uplifting of their people. To this end the training of teachers was considered of the greatest importance. Armstrong believed that the importance of training Indians to teach could not be overemphasized because some of the tribes would soon be thrown on their own resources, having to provide for their own education.

In his first report to the Board of Trustees as principal of the school, Frissell noted that a "number of Indian students are working their way through the school this year without government help in the same way Negro students do. It is desirable that this number be increased." He also mentioned with approval the outing program. "A larger number of our Indians than usual were placed on northern farms last summer. This plan of sending the Indian students out to northern farms, inaugurated by General Armstrong in the summer of 1879 . . . is a most important part of the Indian's education."[56]

But Frissell did not appear to have Armstrong's enthusiasm for the Indian education program. He seemed primarily concerned with the level of preparation of prospective Indian students; Armstrong was interested in educating as many Indians as possible regardless of their academic qualifications. Frissell's position is clearly implied in his 1903 *Annual Report:*

In previous reports the fact has been mentioned that for the past two years no Indians have been received at Hampton except those able to pass the regular entrance examinations, thus doing away with the Indian Preparatory Class. With the increasing number of good schools in the West it seems clear that Hampton ought to receive only those Indians who show some ability as students and some capacity for receiving training as teachers and leaders of their people. Every year there is a struggle for pupils on the part of the principals of the government schools in the West in order to keep their quota. It has not seemed proper that Hampton should enter this struggle. . . .

By raising the standard we have lessened the number of Indians but have greatly improved the quality of material. Unless it is possible to obtain Indians who are capable of meeting its requirements for admission, it seems wise that the school should devote itself more to the education of the Negro and less to that of the Indian.[57]

In the final analysis the only true measure of the effectiveness of Hampton's program for Indians is what they did when they returned to their tribes. Cora M. Folsom gave her opinion: "I consider that a student has made a good record, has done well, when he is industrious, shows a moral and religious uprightness, and makes an intelligent and conscientious use of what advantages he has received." But she also offered some explanatory admonitions as a preface to her follow-up reports on returned Indians after the program had been in operation for twelve years, from 1878 to 1890. "In offering these records to readers unacquainted with Indian life and customs, there are some things that need explanation in order to ensure a just estimate of individual character, as well as the work of education as a whole. The trouble has been, and still is, that too much is commonly expected of these returned students: We require of them more than we would of our own race under similar circumstances, and that is obviously not fair."[58]

According to Folsom's report, the Indians who attended Hampton answered one of the major questions raised at the beginning of the school's educational program for Indians. To the question of the possibility of civilizing Indians, Folsom gave the answer: "There is a great deal said about Indian students going 'back to the blanket,' meaning Indian life. I cannot, of course, speak for students of other schools whom I have not seen, but I do not hesitate to say for *the Hampton students, almost all of whom I have seen,* and for those of other schools whom I have met, that there is no going back to the old way,—to the original starting point."[59] Folsom had visited "almost all" of Hampton's Indian students after they had returned to their tribes. The stated object of the follow-up study was to make "a report as complete as may be of every Indian student who has returned home from Hampton."[60] Her report appears to have achieved this objective, for it contains information concerning 460 returned Indians who had attended Hampton, presumably all such students. Several typical reports on individual returned Indians furnish some insight into the nature of the information collected by Folsom.

Thomas Smith. No wa-tesh, half-blood Gros Ventro, age 15. He was a brother of the Agency Interpreter and spoke some English when he came [to Hampton]. Returned home in '81, found employment as a herder and in 1885 was assistant farmer at the agency. The missionary, Mr. Hall, 1890 reports him as good in character, industry and influence. He himself says "I am wearing citizen's clothes since I left Hampton. I am farming now. I had to rustling to make my living. I have a child. I want him to be in school, and after he grew up, I wanted him to be like white man."

Rosa Pleets, Was'ieuwin, half-blood Sioux, age 15. She returned home from the Indian School [at Hampton] in '81, worked at the Agent's house awhile and then went to live in the family of the missionary, Rev. Mr. Swift, at Moreau River. She came back to Hampton in '84 and remained until '86, when she again returned to Standing Rock and in '87 married John Tiaokasin, one of our students, and came back with him to Hampton a few months later. They remained here, living in a cottage, until '88, then returned to Standing Rock, taking with them their infant son, Richard, then about a year old. They have a pleasant home, a well kept baby and visitors speak of them as examples worthy of imitation. One of the Hampton students writes that he always likes to go to see John and Rosa because "everything is clean; beds, floor, everything is good in their house."

Thomas Wildcat Alford, Kno-ah-pi-ci-ia, a Shawnee from Indian territory, about 19 years of age. He had been to school [at Hampton] before and entered the junior class here, graduating in '82. He returned soon after and has since taught at his home, Shawnee town, and at the Chilocco Industrial School, making six years of continuous and successful teaching. In '88 he gave up his school to assist in the allotment of lands to his tribe. He himself was the first Shawnee to take land in severalty, and has been very earnest and successful in persuading others to follow his example.

Major Poter, special agent for the allotment of land, said of him: "I became acquainted with Thomas Alford, a graduate of Hampton Institute, and John King, and other Hampton students. By their help, after awhile we made four hundred allotments before the appropriation was exhausted. Without the continued assistance of these young men I would have had to return home. They encourage schools, send their relations, and visit the schools themselves several times a year.

"From axeman in the surveyor's corps, Alford soon rose to position of compassman at $4.00 a day, was in '91, the Indian county being thrown open, made a regular surveyor to the county, appointed by the Governor.

"In the intervals of active service, he manages to keep up an excellent plant, has an orchard of 100 fruit trees, 50 acres of fenced

land—30 under cultivation—and pasture for 75 or more head of cat-
tle. . . .

"The neat frame house, log kitchen, stable and sheds were built by
his own hands, and, from the small farm which he manages to keep
up, his table is amply supplied with vegetables, fruits, milk, poultry,
and eggs. . . .

"In '89 I spent several days at this house and found there no want
that industry and intelligence could supply. The house, though small,
was cozy and well appointed. A homemade bookcase, well stocked,
hung on the wall, and beneath it stood a desk so unique as to attact attention at once. This I found to be made from an old sewing machine
frame. . . .

"Character, intelligence and pluck have been rewarded in a most
encouraging way, and the example of this young man's life well done,
and is still doing, much to encourage the Indians among whom he
lives and works. In '92, he wrote, in speaking of General Armstrong's
illness, 'to him we owe all gratitude, all that we are and all the honor.
There are many young men of the plains to-day who praise and thank
God that there are such friends at the East, and that there is such a
school as the Hampton Institute. They may not have appreciated its
benefits while in school, but they have learned to after leaving it.' "[61]

Of course, not every returned Indian student was as successful as the three just mentioned. Certainly Thomas Wildcat Alford approached the complete embodiment of all that
Armstrong and his workers desired for the Indian education
program. Most of Hampton's successful returned Indian
students, like Alford, achieved their goals.

Folsom reported that only 52 of the 460 returned Indians
should be considered as disappointing. Of this number 35 were
rated as poor and 17 as bad when judged by the criteria for success which she established. Thus according to Folsom's reports
over 88 percent of the Indians from Hampton were found to
have done well upon their return to their tribes. Of the 408
whose progress on returning was considered satisfactory, 98
were judged excellent, 219 were good, and 91 were fair.[62] The
program continued to operate successfully until 1912 when, as
we have seen, federal funds were stopped, primarily because of
race problems. A few Indians did continue to enroll to be educated alongside Blacks for years thereafter, but without government support is was only a matter of time before the last Indian

student would depart from the institution. That time came in 1923.

Judged by almost any standards, however exacting, Hampton Institute's Indian education program would have to be judged highly successful. In addition to the advantages gained by the Indian students who attended Hampton, those who attended the off-reservation schools established for Indians also profited from the work done at Hampton. The Hampton Institute program was the model on which off-reservation schools were subsequently patterned. The first such school, located in Carlisle, Pennsylvania, was organized and administered along the lines of Indian education at Hampton. It was founded in 1879 by Captain Pratt, who had brought the first group of Indians to Hampton. Not only did he pattern Carlisle's program after the Hampton plan, but he also had Indian students who had spent a year at Hampton help him get the new school into operation. An observation by no less a person than the president of the United States bears out Hampton's influence on the establishment of the school in Carlisle. In a message to Congress in 1879, President Hayes said: "The experiment of sending a number of Indian children of both sexes to the Hampton Normal and Agricultural Institute in Virginia, to receive an elementary English education and practical instruction in farming and other useful industries, has led to results so promising that it was thought expedient to turn over the calvary barracks at Carlisle in Pennsylvania to the Interior Department, for the establishment of an Indian School on a larger scale."[63]

As was the case with the Carlisle school, other educational institutions were established with government funds, all fashioned after the Hampton Institute model.

Notes

1. This account of the landing of the first party of Indian students at Hampton Institute was reconstructed from numerous accounts of the incident and from drawings, maps, and pictures, Archives, Hampton Institute, Hampton, Va.

2. Samuel Chapman Armstrong to Emma Armstrong, April 15, 1878, Armstrong Collection, Williams College, Williamstown, Mass. *Indians* and *Red men,* the conventional racial designations, will be used throughout this paper even though they are misnomers.

3. "An Indian Raid on Hampton Institute," *Southern Workman* 7 (1878), 36.

4. Joseph Jackson, *The Upward March of the Indian* (Hampton: Hampton Institute Press, 1910), a speech delivered in the Cleveland Hall Chapel at Hampton Institute, Indian Citizenship Day, Feb. 8, 1910.

5. "An Indian Raid," p. 36.

6. Samuel Chapman Armstrong, *Annual Report to the Board of Trustees* (Hampton: Hampton Institute Press, 1878), p. 12 (hereafter cited as *Annual Report* with the year noted).

7. *Annual Report* (1879), p. 11.

8. Ibid. (1879), p. 16.

9. "An Indian Raid," p. 36.

10. Ibid.

11. *Catalogue of Hampton Normal and Agricultural Institute* (Hampton: Hampton Institute Press, 1878), p. 13.

12. "An Indian Raid," p. 36.

13. Ibid.

14. Walton C. John, *Hampton Normal and Agricultural Institute: Its Evolution and Contribution to Education as a Land Grant College,* prepared for Bureau of Education, U.S. Department of Interior, Bulletin no. 27 (Washington, D.C.: Government Printing Office, 1923), p. 89.

15. Ibid.

16. *Annual Report* (1880), p. 12.

17. Samuel Chapman Armstrong, *Annual Report to the Commissioner of Indian Affairs* (Washington, D.C.: Government Printing Office, 1882), p. 7 (hereafter cited as *Annual Report, Indian Affairs* with the year noted).

18. Ibid., p. 8.

19. *Annual Report* (1878), p. 12.

20. *Annual Report* (1882), pp. 3–5.

21. *Annual Report, Indian Affairs* (1882), p. 5.

22. Ibid. (1883), pp. 4–7.

23. *Annual Report* (1880), p. 13.

24. Estelle Reel, "Industrial Training for Indian Children," *Southern Workman* 29 (1900), 201.

25. *Annual Report, Indian Affairs* (1882), p. 3.

26. *Annual Report* (1883), p. 56.

27. Edith Armstrong Talbot, *Samuel Chapman Armstrong: A Biographical Study* (New York: Doubleday Page and Co., 1904), p. 182.

28. M. Friedman, "Religious Work in Indian Schools," *Southern Workman* 37 (1908), 282–84; J. J. Gravatt, "Hampton's Early Days," ibid. 39 (1910), 334–36; and Caroline W. Adrus, "The Indian Convocation at Indian Creek," ibid., pp. 273–76.

29. Talbot, *Armstrong*, p. 211.

30. *Annual Report* (1879), p. 14.

31. Ibid. (1879), p. 36.

32. Ibid. (1881), p. 13.

33. Ibid. (1883). p. 47.

34. Ibid. (1883), p. 39, (1886), p. 12, (1892), p. 23.

35. Ibid. (1879), p. 16.

36. "An Indian Raid," p. 36.

37. *Annual Report, Indian Affairs* (1885), p. 3. Racial designations, including the term *Negro*, were often spelled with lower-case letters.

38. *Report of Commissioner of Indian Affairs* (Washington, D.C.: Government Printing Office, 1880), p. 185.

39. Cora M. Folsom, untitled manuscript (1928), unpaged, Archives, Hampton Institute.

40. "An Indian Raid," p. 36.

41. *Annual Report* (1879), p. 15.

42. *Annual Report, Indian Affairs* (1882), p. 6.

43. Hollis B. Frissell, "Annual Report," *Southern Workman* 41 (1912), 296–97.

44. Helen W. Ludlow, ed. *Ten Years Work for the Indians* (Hampton: Hampton Institute Press, 1888), pp. 12–13.

45. "An Indian Raid," p. 36.

46. *Annual Report* (1897), p. 11.

47. Frissell, "Fifty-fourth Annual Report of the Principal," *Southern Workman* 41 (1912), 297.

48. "The Indian Appropriation," *Southern Workman* 41 (1912), 545–46.

49. John, *Hampton Normal and Agricultural Institute*, p. 89.

50. *Annual Report* (1879), p. 16.

51. Folsom manuscript.

52. *Annual Report, Indian Affairs* (1883), p. 9.

53. Ibid.

54. Talbot, *Armstrong*, p. 157.

55. S. C. Armstrong, "Concerning Indian Education," *Southern Workman* 13 (1884), 44.

56. *Annual Report* (1894), pp. 20, 60.

57. Hollis B. Frissell, "Annual Report," *Southern Workman* 32 (1903), 243–44.

58. *22 Years' Work of Hampton Normal and Agricultural Institute* (Hampton: Hampton Institute Press, 1893), p. 317.

59. Ibid., p. 322.

60. Ibid., p. 316.

61. Ibid., pp. 333–34, 345–46.

62. Ibid., pp. 317–24, 487.

63. Ibid., p. 315.

James A. Garfield and Hampton Institute

Howard V. Young, Jr.

BETWEEN 1870 AND 1930 several men who later became presidents of the United States had close relationships with Hampton Institute. James A. Garfield was the first prominent national political figure to be intimately connected with the school, being one of the incorporators under the Virginia charter of June 1870, serving as a member of the Board of Trustees from 1870 to 1875, and speaking at the Institute both as a congressman in 1872 and as president of the United States in June 1881, just about one month before he was shot in Washington's Union Station.

Garfield's relation to the school developed out of his lifelong interest in, and support of, education. A member of the Disciples of Christ Church, Garfield went to the sect's college at Hiram, Ohio, from 1851 to 1854 and then attended Williams College for two years where he studied under the famous educator Mark Hopkins. He returned to the Western Reserve Eclectic Institute at Hiram as a teacher and became acting head of the school in 1857, when its principal resigned. With the onset of the Civil War in 1861, Garfield, already serving in the state Senate, was elected lieutenant colonel of an Ohio infantry regiment and rapidly rose to the rank of brigadier general. After seeing active service on the western front, he was assigned a position in Washington until he was elected to Congress from Ohio's Nineteenth District as a Republican in 1862. He had been active in politics since the 1856 presidential campaign of John C. Fremont and was noted for his abolitionist beliefs and his advocacy of Black suffrage as early as 1865. A Radical Republican during Reconstruction, he rose rapidly in congressional leadership positions, becoming chairman of the Committee on Military Affairs in 1867, chairman of the Banking and Currency Committee in 1869, and head of the very influential Appropriations Committee in 1874.

Even though he was a conservative in fiscal matters, he was an early advocate of national support to education, and in 1866 at the request of the National Association of School Superintendents he introduced a bill which established the first National Bureau of Education and guided it safely through the House to its final signature by President Andrew Johnson on March 2, 1867.[1] And in 1872 as chairman of the Appropriations Committee he led the unsuccessful fight to have Congress allocate the net proceeds (about $30 million per year) from the sale of public lands for the support of public education in the states. Like many other supporters of Radical Republican Reconstruction in the 1870s, Garfield took refuge in the belief that the effects of a system of universal public education, coupled with business enterprise, would work out the problem of reintegrating the South and its races into the mainstream of the nation.[2]

John Taylor, his most recent biographer, says:

In the United States Congress no one exceeded Garfield in his devotion to education as an ideal. It is hardly surprising that he was much in demand as a commencement speaker and as a sponsor for legislative measures associated with education. But for all his enthusiasm, Garfield's conception of education was a narrow one, one which was closely identified with science and the classics. He was for several years a trustee of Hampton Institute, a newly founded college for Negroes in Norfolk [sic], Virginia, but he soon found himself out of sympathy with the emphasis on vocational education. "Very much manual labor," he wrote on one occasion to a member of the Hampton faculty [General Samuel Chapman Armstrong, the school's principal] "is incompatible with a very high degree of mental cultivation."[3]

Taylor has merely elaborated on the discussion of Garfield's educational philosophy and his relations with Hampton Institute found in the earlier biography by Theodore Clarke Smith:

The next year [1870] Garfield accepted an election to the Board of Trustees, and his correspondence shows him in frequent communication with Armstrong, discussing problems, giving advice and now and then furnishing actual assistance in legal matters. But the impression is created by Garfield's letters that while he theoretically approved of the methods in use at Hampton, the sort of education there given did not, in fact, appeal to his sympathy very strongly. To him education was a matter of high and absorbing aspiration, its goal was the production of scholars, philosophers and scientists, and the problem of laying the foundations for the economic self-support of a dependent race was something wholly different.[4]

This interpretation is a misreading of the available evidence in Garfield's speeches as well as in the correspondence to and from Principal Armstrong. Smith even modifies his own generalizations in the very next paragraph:

Yet two years later, in a letter to Governor Fairchild of Wisconsin (April 19, 1872), he put the case in defense of Armstrong's ideals very clearly. "Whatever doubt there may be," he began, "and I admit there is ground for some, of the success of any manual labor school, it is clear that the first want of the freed people of the South is to know how to live and how to work. And the industrial and agricultural features of the Institution at Norfolk [*sic*], have thus far proved a splendid success in that direction." In addition, he heartily approved the plan of making the school a normal one for the furnishing of colored teachers, of the custom of giving special instruction to the more intelligent, and finally the location of the school actually among the colored people.[5]

The more specialized study by Burke A. Hinsdale concludes that Garfield, though a student of the classics and a teacher, also saw that the enormous extension of knowledge, the growth of modern literature, and the development of industry called for a widely differentiated education. The "new education" took a strong hold on his mind and he favored a revision of the traditional classical course. He said Greek and Latin must give way.[6]

This view was substantiated as early as Garfield's speech before the literary societies of Hiram College, on June 14, 1867, in which he condemned, not just criticized, current education as being unrealistic in fitting a person for contemporary life because it taught nothing about the "laws of life and physical well being" or about agriculture. He said that the scholar and the worker must join hands in the educational system if both were to be successful.[7]

Biographers Smith and Taylor have patently ignored the superb summary of Garfield's advanced educational philosophy contained in his address "College Education," the main points of which are essential for an understanding of his real views. Garfield said that there are two purposes of all study: "to discipline our faculties and to acquire knowledge for the duties for life." Higher education should include instruction in the nature of the human body and how to preserve one's health, in the history of the nation and the workings of the government, in the development of a philosophy of life, and up-to-date instruction in one's chosen profession. His last point is particularly germane to his relations with Hampton Institute. He held that each student should be taught modern science and develop an acquaintance with modern industry through a program of manual labor.

I am well aware of the current notion that these muscular arts should stay in the fields and shops, and not invade the sanctuaries of learning. A finished education is supposed to consist mainly of literary culture. . . . This generation is beginning to understand that education should not be forever divorced from industry, that the highest results can be reached only when science guides the hand of labor. With what eagerness and alacrity is industry seizing every truth of science, and putting it in harness?[8]

He concluded that "our colleges have done, and are doing a noble work, for which they deserve the thanks of the nation; but he is not their enemy who suggests that they ought to do much better." And as a member of the Hiram College Board of Trustees he made the surprise announcement in 1867 to the students that the Board of Trustees had just voted to make the classics elective rather than required subjects. Pleased that Harvard University had just reduced the amount of required Greek and Latin by two thirds, he stated: "I rejoice that the movement has begun. Other colleges must follow the example; and the day will not be far distant when it shall be the pride of a scholar that he is also a worker, and when the worker shall not refuse to become a scholar because he despises a trifler."[9]

Although Garfield was a classical scholar, these remarks alone indicate that he realized the practical limitations of the

classics and that he was much more sympathetic toward the new
Hampton system than these biographers have indicated. What
was the new curriculum of Hampton? In October 1873, shortly
after the school opened, teacher Helen Ludlow wrote a descriptive article in *Harper's Magazine* stating that the school's purpose
was to offer "an opportunity to earn at once a solid English
education and a valuable industrial training. Reading, spelling, writing and grammar are carried through the entire
course—along with the principles of natural science, book-
keeping, drawing and music. The senior class studies geometry,
mechanics, physiology, English history and literature and the
outlines of universal history, the science of civil government
and moral science [philosophy]. Each student works on the
farm one day a week and on Saturday morning to earn their
board."[10] Thus this program fits the very reforms of American
education which Garfield put forth six years before in his
speech "College Education."

It is also important to note under what circumstances
Garfield's letter of September 27, 1870, was written since these
biographers have misinterpreted it. After Garfield agreed to
serve on the Board of Trustees, Armstrong tried repeatedly to
get him more involved in the school's affairs by urging him to
attend one of the Trustees' meetings. Then in a letter of
August 11, 1870, Armstrong asked Garfield to "draw up a
prospectus of the Institute that will embrace the whole of its
work." Armstrong confessed that he had tried to "get up one"
but was not satisfied and thought Garfield could write a better
one: "You have more perfectly than the rest of us the idea of
what is to be done in this way."[11]

But Garfield's forthcoming election campaign prevented him
from accepting this task and even from making the dedicatory
address for the new academic building to be consecrated on
October 14. So Armstrong had to undertake "an outline of the
work before us" which he sent to the congressman on September 13, 1870, asking him "to correct it."[12] Garfield wrote
from his home in Hiram, Ohio, that he found Armstrong's
paper "helpful." He had only this reservation:

I would not, if I were in your place, commit myself absolutely to the
policy of manual labor schools—as a principle of general application

for the reason that hitherto all such experiments have finally failed and for the stronger reason that very much manual labor is inconsistent with a very high degree of mental culture. If you have not already read it, please read Elliott's [Charles W. Eliot] paper in the *Atlantic Monthly* for February 1869 particularly the first half of page 287 where he discusses this topic. This and one other article on the same subject made him president of Harvard. While I endorse this view as a general principle, and fully and cordially support the labor feature of your school as the proper course at least for the present, I defend it on the ground of the peculiar and exceptional situation in which we find the colored race of the South. The question is how best to lead them up from the plane of mere drudgery to one of [*illegible*] of high culture, so the labor system is the most excellent bridge to carry them over the intermediate or transitional period. . . . you will find that the labor feature is less and less needed as the race rises in the [*illegible*] of culture and that by and by they will require a course [?] nearer the ordinary college than they now do.[13]

He suggested that Armstrong base his "defense of the labor feature more on the special situation of the race than on general principles and that we do not commit ourselves to the doctrine that we may hereafter be required to retract and apologize."[14] At the end of this very cordial response to Armstrong's invitation to "correct" his prospectus, Garfield half apologized for his suggestions; and it is certainly a misinterpretation of Garfield's whole educational outlook and his relationship to Hampton to indicate that his reservations about manual labor in the Institute's program led to his severing his relations with it by resigning from the Board of Trustees five years later.

If Garfield held the views attributed to him by Smith and Taylor, why would he have written Armstrong in April 1870 that "I am glad to hear of the fine prospects of our Institution at Hampton and whenever any opportunity occurs where I can strike a blow for it I shall be glad to do so"? This exchange of letters certainly does not represent any confrontation of views between Garfield and Armstrong or any parting of the ways because of incompatible educational philosophies, for Armstrong heartily thanked Garfield on October 3, 1870, for his "kind suggestions" and added "I think they are right and that it altogether wise . . . as you say by not committing ourselves to perpetual manual labor."[15]

On December 3, 1872, Garfield wrote the principal: "I am much gratified to hear of the great prosperity of the Institute at Hampton. No Institution thrives unless it has a principle of life in itself. Yours meets a great and pressing want among the colored people and as its work is pushed with vigor and sense, responses come in students."[16] And when President Garfield spoke in Bethesda Chapel at Hampton on June 5, 1881, to the Black and newly arrived Indian students, he stressed that their future lay in acquiring the habit of work, for although labor must be free,

LABOR MUST BE!—for you, for all.—Without it there can be no civilization. The white race has learned that truth. They came here as pioneers, felled the forests and swept away all obstacles before them by labor. You come from a people who have been taught to destroy;—to fight but not to labor. Therefore to you I would say that without labor you can be nothing. The first text in your civilization is; Labor must be!

Bethesda Chapel, near Hampton Institute, where President James A. Garfield spoke on June 5, 1881

You of the African race have learned this text but you learned it under the lash. Slavery taught you that labor must be. The mighty voice of war spoke out to you, and to us all, that Labor must be forever FREE.

The basis of all civilization is that Labor must be. The basis of every thing great in civilization, the glory of our civilization, is that Labor must be free!

I am glad to see that General Armstrong is working out this problem on both sides—reaching one hand to the South; and one hand to the West,—with all this Continent of Anglo-Saxon civilization behind him; working it out in the only way it can ever be worked out; the way that will give us a country without sections; a people without a stain.[17]

Garfield's philosophy of education corresponded to Hampton's. But Garfield first became interested in Hampton Institute as a result of his friendships with General O. O. Howard, head of the Freedman's Bureau, and Mark Hopkins, president of Williams College, both of whom were also friends of General Armstrong. Garfield and Hopkins visited Hampton in July 1869 along with Dr. Strieb, the senior secretary of the American Missionary Association, to consult with Armstrong about his building plans. They seemingly favored the purchase of the Chesapeake Female Seminary but were persuaded by Armstrong's forceful, almost stubborn, desire to build a new academic building on the property along Hampton Creek.[18]

Along with General Howard, Garfield was one of the original trustees of Hampton Institute listed in the charter granted by an act of the Virginia General Assembly June 4, 1870. Between January 1870 and July 1881, the principal and the congressman exchanged at least 110 letters. Throughout the spring of 1870 Armstrong was concerned that the Virginia legislature, dominated by white conservatives, would change Hampton's original charter, granted by the Elizabeth City County Circuit Court; he feared they would restrict enrollment of Blacks by striking out the phrase "without distinction of color" in reference to the future student body.[19] Several times Armstrong consulted Garfield, who was counted as one of the more influential Radical Republican congressmen, on how to counteract the conservative drive against the school's interracial charter. He assured Garfield that the Radicals in the Virginia House of Delegates would be guided by the congressman's advice—which was finally to drop the whole matter and get Hampton incorporated under the General Incorporation Act.[20] But this proved unnecessary as the legislature finally agreed to approve the charter as originally written.

Armstrong also consulted Garfield about the division of the proceeds from the sale of public lands under the Morrill Act for the support of education.[21] This was finally settled much to Hampton's advantage when the state of Virginia voted one third of its share of the "Land Script" to Hampton Institute.[22]

Armstrong wanted to have Garfield act as a public champion of the school and assist in his running battle with the American Missionary Association trustees who exerted authority because they founded Hampton and appointed Armstrong.[23] The principal was constantly devising ways to involve Garfield more actively in Hampton's affairs. Besides asking his advice on legislative strategy, Armstrong tried desperately to get Garfield to come to the Board of Trustees' meetings. And he also occasionally asked for Garfield's aid in getting money for Hampton from various agencies of the federal government. Trying to finish Academic Hall in the spring of 1870 and being at the end of his funds, Armstrong literally begged Garfield to see General Howard personally and have him cash a check for $4,-000 on Freedman's Bureau funds.[24] Garfield performed this errand, but evidently General Howard could not advance that amount from these residual monies.

At its November 1870 meeting the Board of Trustees resolved to ask a committee of four members, taken in alphabetical order, to visit the school annually in turn, and to make a report back to the trustees. Armstrong almost gleefully informed Garfield that along with Holmes, Howard, and Hyde he was on the first committee to be chosen for this task. Garfield subsequently agreed, but he would not promise to visit Hampton unless he was sure Armstrong would be there, and not on one of his fund-raising trips.[25]

Of necessity Armstrong also had many dealings with the officials in charge of the nearby National Asylum for Disabled

Volunteer Soldiers and in December 1870 asked Garfield to consult with General Butler, national president of the Veterans' Asylums, about appointing a Mr. White as superintendent. General Butler said that he did not intend appointing a superintendent at that time but would consult with Armstrong when the number of inmates got large enough to warrant such an official. In the meantime the chaplain would continue to administer the facility. The principal again asked Garfield to attend a meeting of the Virginia Senate with him in February 1871, where the division of the state's land funds would be voted upon in order to "impress on these Republicans the importance of their duty" as they were "a slightly uncertain set and have to be taught their duty with as much force and clearness as possible." But on this and later occasions Garfield did not have the time to come down to Richmond, and he also questioned the wisdom of appearing before the legislature's conservative-dominated committees because his reputation as a Radical Republican might prejudice the case for Hampton. As his letter to Armstrong shows, Garfield did his most effective work for Hampton in Washington, such as convincing General Howard to vest the legal title to the buildings at Hampton Institute in the hands of the trustees.[26]

Garfield's second visit to Hampton came on March 9, 1872, as part of General Butler's inspecting party for the National Asylum for Disabled Volunteer Soldiers. At Armstrong's behest, Garfield had invited this official party to tour Hampton Institute. Garfield and his wife even returned from Fort Monroe later in the day to spend the night with the Armstrongs. At 8 A.M. the principal took the Garfields in his yacht back to Fort Monroe, where the whole party caught the steamer *Lady of the Lake* for Washington. He was not to return to Hampton until 1881.[27]

In the course of his correspondence with Garfield, the principal revealed his political concerns and views as he sought Garfield's trust, confidence, and action on behalf of Hampton Institute.[28] At first, as an abolitionist and antisecessionist—a fervent Radical Republican—Armstrong was concerned with how the Republican Party could stay in power in the South. He hoped Garfield's current appropriation bill would provide liberally for the South because enlarging the new state school system was the only means of "avoiding the loss of the Negro vote to the Republican Party . . . and yet many Republicans from the South find their best chance for reelection to Congress in the continued ignorance of Negroes so that they can again work upon colored men's prejudices and secure their votes." In August 1870 he asked: "Does not the loss of North Carolina . . . [by] the Republicans make it clear that without a very great and national effort at education, in the South, it will be lost also? There is no other way of salvation—politically—than through the spelling book."[29]

Like Garfield, Armstrong shortly thereafter came to believe that military reconstruction of the South was not working because of increasing northern apathy about the Black man's plight and massive and violent southern white resistance to Black political participation. Armstrong expressed his doubts pithily: "I hope it will at least be seen that school teachers are needed now just as much as bayonets were once, and that Congress will adopt an extensive, powerful system of Southern schools as far as that is possible."[30]

On the other hand, in keeping with his belief that southerners were more sincerely interested in Blacks than northerners were and knew even better the extent of their capabilities than Blacks themselves,[31] Armstrong often assured Garfield that the sentiment of the "best Virginian is most heartily with us" and that "our relations with this state are most satisfactory." In December 1872 the principal claimed, "I am personally on the pleasantest terms with the Southern white [*illegible*] classes but they in their inmost hearts hate to see the darkey come up. Yet they are outwardly not opposed but in favor of his education as a necessity to prevent them stealing."[32] As a congressman, Garfield may have been a Radical Republican in the 1860s, but by the time he became a member and then chairman of the powerful House Appropriations Committee in the early 1870s he was an avowed fiscal conservative. He was opposed to President Grant's plan to employ unemployed laborers on public works during the very bad depression starting in 1873, and only grudgingly agreed that the government would probably have to give some aid to the victims of a major

Mississippi River flood.[33] He was therefore less than enthusiastic about supporting Armstrong's many appeals for
federal grants to aid Hampton, though occasionally he gave
Armstrong some encouragement: "It may be possible that
something can be done in Congress though I am not sure if
there are any funds left of the Freedman's Bureau property
perhaps that might be used. I will look over the matter fully
and see what the possibilities are."[34]

In December 1872, when Armstrong was made desperate by
housing conditions that witnessed twenty-five male students being quartered in tents in bitterly cold winter weather, he wrote
the congressman asking whether there were any funds arising
from unpaid bounties and arrears of colored soldiers or of
colored deserters which could be used to build a dormitory at
Hampton since the funds would be used for the education of
the children of colored soldiers. But finally he seems to have
realized that no money would be available from federal
largesse, and when he planned to see Garfield in Washington in
mid-December 1873, he exulted that "we are fortunate. A
gentleman of Boston says, 'Put up the new building at once and
I'll pay the bills.'"[35]

Garfield philosophically supported Hampton's plan of
combining manual labor training with academic work, but he
did not take an active part in Hampton's educational program
and did not come to the Trustee meetings because he was so
thoroughly tied up on several important House committees.
Garfield also had to refuse many opportunities for other kinds
of travel as well. He had to pass up congressional junkets, like
the trip to a "Congressional Convention" in Saint Louis, in May
1873, which was designed to influence members of Congress to
vote funds for improving the navigation of the Mississippi
River.[36] And when, for example, he was invited by the secretary
of the navy to accompany him to Norfolk on June 5, 1874, he
could not get away because of his work as chairman of the Appropriations Committee.

The resignation of Garfield from the Board of Trustees
came about under amicable circumstances that did not cool his
interest in, or inhibit his actions on behalf of, Hampton Institute. The congressman had never attended any of the

Trustee meetings despite constant personal appeals from Armstrong, and after another such failure to show up at the 1874 annual meeting, the principal wrote him a warning note: "It is so long since you have been at a meeting that the orthodox fathers [of the American Missionary Association] begin to want to know about it. I hope there is a prospect that you can get hold of this school for you can be of great use to it."[37] On June 14, 1875, after Garfield had missed another annual meeting, the principal wrote:

I have been very discouraged at your not having been at either of the five last annual meetings of our Board of Trustees. We are always bothered to get a quorum and we want just such experience and power you have active in our board. . . . This is not good for the school and I am now writing this situation to those who have been most absent that they either attend or withdraw. We need a man like you in public position but we need more good care on the interests of the school.

I am very anxious to have able men take hold here and you could, had you had time, or had it been possible, have done valuable work for us. I am very sorry to write in this way but I think I ought to.

Yours sincerely,
S. C. Armstrong[38]

Garfield responded shortly and officially tendered his resignation because "I find it so difficult to attend meetings of the Board." But he accompanied this missive with a personal note of explanation to Armstrong:

I returned to this city day before yesterday, after an absence of two months in California. I was so completely overworked by the last session that I was compelled to get away from all employment to recuperate.

Your letter of the 14th came to hand last evening. You are wholly right in the position you take with regard to . . . trustees, and I owe you and the Institute many apologies for having so long failed [illegible] to attend meetings of the Trustees, but from unavoidable engagements. I ought long ago to have resigned, for no man ought to hold a place the duties of which he cannot perform.

I enclose, herewith, my resignation and assure you that I shall feel just the same interest in the Institution as though I continued to be a member of the Board. If at any time I am able to visit you, I shall certainly do so.

As ever yours,

J. A. Garfield[39]

As early as January 31, 1876, Armstrong returned to his old attempt to get Garfield and his wife to visit Hampton and address "our students and the public, say on the Centennial—we need stirring up—not an elaborate speech—just on any national topic. I want you to see the school and its growth. Bring some good man with you from Congress, anyone you like." And the principal still confided in him: "There are several trustees who ought to resign and do not; they are doing nothing and never attend and have no . . . value. By your resignation I get a leverage on them. It is disgusting how men of 'piety' will put themselves in the way of good work."[40] As soon as Garfield was inaugurated president of the United States, Armstrong asked him for a policy statement on the education of Indians in "manual labor schools at the South" which could be read at a fund-raising meeting to be held in New York on March 15, designed to secure $20,000 for the erection of a building to house the Indian girls at Hampton.[41]

Garfield did not forget Hampton even in his first days as president. The Hampton Institute Cadets, 101 men with a band of 13 pieces, were invited to march in Garfield's inaugural parade on March 4, 1881. They went up to Washington by steamer overnight on the third, stayed in Howard University's Chapel, and joined the line of march the next day, but were so far from the Capitol that they could not hear the president's address.[42] He touched briefly on the degenerating status of Black people: "Under our institutions there is no middle ground for the negro between slavery and equal citizenship. There can be no permanent disfranchised peasantry in the United States." He also advocated universal public education—by national, state and volunteer forces—to overcome mass illiteracy, but he did not propose any specific program of federal aid to public education, as he had done when he was a congressman in 1872—or any way to reverse the movement to the solid Democratic South.[43]

Armstrong visited Garfield in the White House to make final
arrangements for the president's projected visit to Hampton
for the annual Anniversary Exercise in 1881, but Garfield
could not get away until early June.[44] Finally, on Saturday,
June 4, 1881, President Garfield, his son and daughter, and a
small official party arrived from Washington on the steam
yacht *Dispatch* and visited Fort Monroe and the Portsmouth
Navy Yard. On Sunday morning they drove to the National
Asylum for Disabled Volunteer Soldiers and Hampton Institute and attended church at Bethesda Chapel in the National
Cemetery along with Union veterans and Hampton's Black and
recently arrived Indian students. After the religious service,
Armstrong announced the presence of the president and
expressed the hope that he would speak to the school "of which
he had so long been a friend and was once a Trustee, in this
most fitting place, with the graves around us of those who have
died that these might be here today." Then President Garfield
spoke in turn to each of the three groups in the chapel, referring to the veterans as representing the past and the students
the future. He stressed the necessity and value of labor in building successful lives for the Black and Indian peoples.[45] Evidently the president had a high regard for his speech at
Bethesda Chapel, for he wrote Armstrong on June 9 to request
that he find out if someone had taken notes. The president had
heard that a shorthand reporter from one of the Boston papers
had been present, and he asked Armstrong to send him a copy
if it were available.[46] Garfield was shot less than a month later,
on July 2, 1881, and died on September 19.

Armstrong was almost desperately anxious to have Garfield
take an active part in building Hampton Institute because of his
sincere interest in, and knowledge of, contemporary American
education. But because of his prior commitment to his political
career, the congressman and future president was unable to
fulfill this role in Hampton's development. Nevertheless, until
1875 Garfield's correspondence with Armstrong provided important psychological assistance to the struggling school principal; and as an influential Republican politician and
congressman, Garfield was able to help the school get some
financial aid. But one is left saddened as much by the blighted

prospects of a Hampton built with the active cooperation of Garfield and Armstrong as by the untimely end of Garfield's own life and career at the hands of an assassin.

Notes

1. *The Works of James Abram Garfield,* ed. Burke A. Hinsdale (Boston: James R. Osgood and Co., 1882), 1: 126–42.

2. *The Diaries of James Garfield,* with an Introduction by Harry James Brown and Frederick D. Williams (East Lansing: Michigan State University Press, 1967), vol. 1, *1848–1871,* p. x1 (hereafter cited as *Garfield Diary*).

3. John M. Taylor, *Garfield of Ohio: The Available Man* (New York: W. W. Norton and Co., 1970), pp. 156–57.

4. *Life and Letters of James Abram Garfield* (New Haven: Yale University Press, 1925), 2:803.

5. Ibid., p. 804.

6. *President Garfield and Education* (Boston: James R. Osgood and Co., 1882), pp. 253–56.

7. Garfield, "College Education" (address), in Hinsdale, ed., *Works,* 1:271.

8. Ibid., pp. 266, 269–70.

9. Ibid., pp. 276, 282–83.

10. Helen W. Ludlow, "The Hampton Normal and Agricultural Institute," *Harper's New Monthly Magazine* 47 (1873), 681.

11. Aug. 11, 1870, Garfield Papers, ser. 4, vol. 17, item 36, Manuscripts Division, Library of Congress.

12. Sept. 13, 1870, ibid., ser. 4, vol. 17, item 131.

13. Sept. 27, 1870, ibid., ser. 6A, vol. 6, pp. 150–52. Parts of this letter are illegible, but the major points Garfield made are clear.

14. Ibid., p. 152.

15. April 11, 1870, ibid., ser. 6A, vol. 5, p. 103; Oct. 3, 1870, ibid., ser. 4, vol. 17, item 204.

16. Dec. 3, 1872, ibid., ser. 6A, vol. 12, p. 27.

17. "Hampton Notes," *Southern Workman* 10 (1881), 74.

18. Edith Armstrong Talbot, *Samuel Chapman Armstrong: A Biographical Study* (New York: Doubleday, Page and Co., 1904), p. 174.

19. May 13, 1870, Garfield Papers, ser. 4, vol. 15, item 169; April 30, 1870, ibid., ser. 4, vol. 15, item 111.

20. May 3, 1870, Garfield Papers, ser. 6A, vol. 5, page 241.

21. May 18, 1870, Garfield Papers, ser. 4, vol. 15, item 198.

22. Robert Francis Engs, "The Development of Black Culture and Community in Hampton Roads, Virginia, 1861–1870," Diss. Yale 1972, p. 196.

23. December 10, 1870, Garfield Papers, ser. 4, vol. 18, item 79. Armstrong reported: "Had trustee meeting Nov. 17th (1870) with good at-

tendance and transacted lots of business and wound up with a set-to on the property question in which I went at the A.M. Associate Secretaries (who were present) as strongly as I could. . . . They have agreed to turn over the property but insist that the trustees shall first secure $30,000 [either for endowment or as a building fund, evidently]. I ridiculed this idea. But they held out. I wanted you badly. You'd have used them up."

24. May 13, 1870, Garfield Papers, ser. 4, vol. 15, item 169.

25. Dec. 12, 1870, ibid., ser. 4, vol. 18, item 128; Dec. 13, 1870, ibid., ser. 6A, vol. 6, p. 374. The dates are correct. This exchange of letters within little more than one day is not at all atypical of the rapidity with which the mail was delivered a century ago and certainly reinforces one's view of the inadequacy of our present postal system.

26. Dec. 1, 1870, ibid., ser. 4, vol. 18, item 79; Dec. 23, 1870, ibid., ser. 6A, vol. 6, page 435; Feb. 8, 1871, ibid., ser. 4, vol. 20, item 78; Feb. 11, 1871, ser. 4, vol. 20, item 92; July 13, 1871, ibid., ser. 6A, vol. 8, pp. 493–94; April 17, 1871, ibid., ser. 6A, vol. 7, pp. 336–39.

27. Entries of March 9 and March 10, 1872, and n. 104, *Garfield Diary*, vol. 2, *1872–1874*, pp. 28–29.

28. Garfield Papers, ser. 4, vol. 21, item 20. Armstrong said "I want you to be a power in our school; the [American Missionary Association] trustees will mostly be negative—some of them neither useful nor ornamental."

29. Jan. 15, 1870, ibid., ser. 4, vol. 14, item 42; Aug. 11, 1870, ibid., ser. 4, vol. 17, item 30.

30. Ibid., ser. 4, vol. 17, item 30.

31. Engs, "Development of Black Culture and Community," p. 197.

32. March 4, 1871, Garfield Papers, ser. 4, vol. 20, item 233; April 4, 1871, ibid., ser. 4, vol. 28, item 197.

33. Entries of Dec. 4 and Dec. 7, 1874, *Garfield Diary*, 2:399–400; June 1, 1874, 2:331.

34. Dec. 3, 1872, Garfield Papers, ser. 6A, vol. 12, p. 27.

35. Dec. 8, 1872, ibid., ser. 4, vol. 28, item 197; Dec. 11, 1873, ibid., ser. 4, vol. 33, item 159.

36. Entries for May 13, 1873, and June 4, 1874, *Garfield Diary*, 2:179, 333.

37. May 20, 1874, Garfield Papers, ser. 4, vol. 36, item 70.

38. June 14, 1875, ibid., ser. 4, vol. 36, item 70.

39. June 18, 1875, ibid., ser. 6A, vol. 17, pp. 253, 257.

40. Jan. 31, 1876, ibid., ser. 4, vol. 41, item 241; Feb. 12, 1876, ibid., ser. 4, vol. 41, item 256.

41. March 7, 1881, ibid., ser. 4, vol. 133, item 539. These funds were evidently designed to erect the original Winona Hall.

42. "Hampton Notes," *Southern Workman* 10 (1881), 44.

43. Rayford Logan, *Betrayal of the Negro* (New York: Collier-Macmillan, 1965), p. 49.

44. May 5, 1881, Garfield Papers, ser. 4, vol. 139, item 170, p. 49.

45. "Hampton Notes," *Southern Workman* 10 (1881), 74.

46. June 9, 1881, Garfield Papers, ser. 6A, vol. 20, p. 355.

Projections, Projects, and Finance:
The Letters of Hollis Burke Frissell
Charles D. Walters

EARLY IN THE EVENING in Hampton, 1894, one could see Principal Hollis B. Frissell with his stiff collar getting on the electric car to go down to catch the night steamer for New York City or Baltimore. His entourage would include the vocal quintet, dressed in their military cadet uniforms, and two beautiful young women, one Black and the other Indian. They could expect to be in the North for several weeks going from New York City to Boston to Buffalo and Albany, holding meetings in churches to raise money to keep Hampton Institute open. The quintet would sing spirituals and hymns at the meetings, and the young women would give readings and tell of the work being done at Hampton. Always frugal, Frissell and his students traveled at reduced rates because he was on missionary work. The programs to uplift the students, the projects he envisaged, and especially the money to finance them—these were Frissell's constant concerns.

The early years after the death of Samuel Chapman Armstrong in 1893 were demanding and perplexing for Principal Frissell because much of the money attracted by the prestige of the Armstrong family stopped coming to the school. On November 30, 1894, he wrote: "Our financial outlook is rather dark and we must look to the friends of these two races to see that Hampton receives the needed support."[1] And a week later he sounded even more disheartened: "There has never been a time when the collection came in so slowly as this fall."[2] Frissell was still hard pressed to find the necessary money the next year: "The difficulties of meeting the expenses of this institution since the death of General Armstrong have been so great that I have been obliged to devote myself summer and winter to the task of raising funds."[3] The years between 1893 and 1895 were extremely difficult for Principal Frissell as he was learning how to run the school and making new contacts as

Hollis Burke Frissell, principal of Hampton Institute (1893–1917)

well as reacquainting the many friends of the Armstrong family with the ever-growing financial problems of the institution. By 1896, however, his letters reflect his optimism and indicate that he had solved many of the problems and was ready to offer additional programs to more students. "We are fearfully poor but we are trying to keep up good courage," he wrote in autumn of 1896, showing again the determination and commitment to both students and supporters.[4] "We are doing all that we can here to make good and intelligent citizens of our students, as we feel that only in that way can the generosity of Hampton's friends be repaid."[5]

Neither defeated nor painfully discouraged by these financial difficulties, Principal Frissell continued to write a tremendous number of letters to contacts in this country as well as in Great Britain and France, devoting the majority of his work during his first five years as principal to raising money to cover his plans to expand the trade school and to open a normal school to an ever-increasing number of students. He was a master letterwriter and took great pains to overlook no detail or contact for funds. He always thanked the group or individual for the money and wrote long personal letters, whether to a Sunday school class in New York thanking them for their $1.07 contribution or to the directors of the Slater Fund thanking them for $15,000.00.

By 1898 Principal Frissell had developed seven form letters that he sent out to long lists of people throughout the world. The seven form letters, with slight variations, are substantially alike and sound the identical theme. Form letter no. 1 reads:

You have doubtless heard of Hampton Institute and its work for the Indians and negroes. This school founded by General Armstrong soon after the close of the war, has always upheld industrial education as the surest means of fitting these people for useful citizenship. The success of Hampton methods is best shown by the work that is being done by her graduates, most notable among whom is Booker T. Washington, Principal of Tuskegee School in Alabama.

Unable with their present training to compete with white mechanics, the blacks are being pushed out from shops both north and south, and as freemen are losing their hold on the trades they practiced in slavery. If this is to be prevented, members of their own race must be trained as industrial leaders and teachers who shall open shops of their own, build decent homes, cultivate the land properly.

From its farms and sixteen shops, Hampton has already sent out many such leaders, but more and better trained mechanics are necessary. To promote this end, the Slater Fund Board of Trustees has promised $6,000 a year for at least five years, with a probable increase afterwards, towards carrying on a trade school at Hampton. Mr. Morris K. Jessup of New York has contributed $10,000 for a building to be known as the Armstrong and Slater Memorial Trade School Building, and other friends have increased the sum to $26,000. The work of erection is far advanced, but in order to complete the building and prepare it for class work, $14,000 more is needed.

We should be very glad to have your help in this enterprise, which we believe deserving of your support, and which we trust will promote the best interests, not only of the Indian and negro races, but also of our country. Bishop Potter of New York, in speaking of Hampton has said, "There are philanthropies of which one may be excused for being in some doubt, but this is not one of them."[6]

Letters thanking citizens for their contributions, mailed within a month after the form letter was sent, indicate that Frissell was successful in raising the money he needed to expand and maintain Hampton Institute.

At the same time, Frissell mailed a slightly longer, more detailed version of the appeal, emphasizing the program's accomplishments:

We desire to bring to your attention the claims of the Hampton Institute, which in its work of educating young people of the negro and Indian races, is devoting special attention to instruction in trades and manual training.

This institution, incorporated under the laws of Virginia, is controlled by a Board of seventeen Trustees, composed of men well known in business and professional circles, representing six different religious denominations, who have managed its property so skillfully that there has not only been no loss through the last three years of financial stress, but an increase in its funds. It receives help from the state for its agricultural work, and from the general government towards the education of the Indians.

The results of its training are shown in the lives and work of such men as Mr. Booker T. Washington of Tuskegee, and the forty graduates it has sent to aid him, as well as by hundreds of others who are helping to improve the material, moral and intellectual conditions of the negroes of the south and the Indians of the west.

The school with its sixteen shops, saw-mill and farm, has sent out many industrial leaders trained under the old apprenticeship system, who have at the same time earned their board and learned their trades in the productive industries of the institute.

But a greater demand than ever is upon is. There is a call for more and better equipped mechanics in the south. If the blacks are to hold their own in the trade, Hampton must train and send out more men capable of opening shops and employing black labor. Unless this is done the negroes will lose the best heritage of slavery—opportunity to work at trades—an opportunity which is for the most part denied them in the north.

Realizing the importance of this matter, the Board of Trustees of the John F. Slater Fund, promised $6,000 annually toward the support of a trade school at Hampton, on condition that a suitable building should be provided for the purpose. Such a building with ten large rooms, has already been partially completed and equipped, and over a hundred young men are receiving instruction in carpentering, wheel-wrighting, blacksmithing, painting, brick-laying, and plastering, the machinist's trade and in mechanical drawing. $37,000 of the $45,000 needed to complete and equip the building has already been paid in. Mr. Morris K. Jessup of New York has contributed $10,000 of this amount, and three ladies in Philadelphia $20,000; but there is immediate need of $8,000 more.

If the negroes and Indians are to be uplifted, they must have trained mechanical and agricultural leaders, and we respectfully ask that you give your support to this most important work, which has so thoroughly won the confidence of this country, and which is in urgent need of funds to complete and carry out the plans of its great founder, General Armstrong.[7]

In this form letter Frissell again names prominent persons, but in order to emphasize Hampton's legitimacy he also states that it was incorporated under the laws of Virginia and that the institute received aid from the state as well as from the federal government. Highlighting the program's varied areas and its development, the additional details in this letter were perhaps based on the aphoristic notion that success breeds success. The appeal is sophisticated and effective; Frissell's success is documented in his annual reports.

Hollis Burke Frissell had come a long way from the days when he commuted from Bergen, New Jersey, to New York City each day to attend school and to work afternoons and weekends. President Edwin A. Alderman of the University of Virginia made the following statement concerning President Frissell in the November 1917 issue of the *Southern Workman:* "No man in American public life, I dare to say, has done more to heal the wounds of war, to bind the sections together, to unify the nation, to build up a finer and free civilization on the ruins of an old order, than this unobtrusive missionary to a backward race."[8]

In his *Education for Life: The Story of Hampton Institute,* F. G. Peabody gives us a clear picture of the developmental years of Frissell.[9]

He was born on July 14, 1851, in South Amenia, New York, one of three boys and one girl, to the Presbyterian Minister Amasa Frissell and the former Lavinia Barker. By saving his money, he was able to enter Phillips Academy in Andover, Massachusetts, for one year before entering Yale University in 1869. He worked his way through college by waiting on tables and singing in the Synagogue. He graduated one year late in 1874 because he had to drop out of school when he contracted a serious case of typhoid fever. He worked as a submaster of a private boarding school in Rhinebech on the Hudson, New York, for two years before entering Union Theological Seminary in 1876. During the time he attended seminary, he worked as an assistant to Charles Robinson, pastor of the Madison Avenue Presbyterian Church, New York City.

A prospective chaplain, Frissell was invited to deliver a sermon at Hampton Institute in 1880. As he delivered the sermon on the grounds of the National Cemetery, his notes blew away in a gust of wind. He completed his sermon, however, and thus began his long association with General Armstrong and Hampton Institute.

Frissell became more than a chaplain when he was appointed vice-principal in 1886. While serving in this capacity, which he held until the death of Armstrong, when he became principal, he developed his extraordinary ability as innovator, administrator, and crusader for education. He became deeply concerned with the education of Negroes and Indians and, as a consequence, participated actively in rebuilding the educational system in the South for children of both races. During this time he invited leaders from all parts of the nation to visit and observe the work at Hampton Institute, and he also began to hold educational conferences on the campus each summer.

Principal Frissell was an innovator in curriculum. His many fund-raising letters to both individuals and associations stated his views on the program at Hampton. Several of his letters indicate his strong feelings about the need for a sound vocational education for Blacks. To a Miss Cope he stressed "the practical, industrial training given here" as "the most important part of the school life of our students."[10] He looked optimistically to the benefits of the trade school: "The outlook at present seems bright and hopeful, and we expect to be able to start a Trade School in the fall which will improve very much the facilities for thorough, practical instruction in the various industries taught here."[11] And further, he saw Hampton's graduates continuing its programs when they returned home, not merely as skilled tradesmen but as teachers ready to impart their acquired knowledge and as moral examples whose conduct would spread through entire communities. "The object of Hampton School is to train earnest young men and women of the Indian and negro races to be the teachers and industrial leaders of their people. We endeavor to fit them for work among those of their own race who are living in ignorance, poverty, and superstition all through the south and west."[12]

Indeed, convinced of the efficacy of such practical training, he urged the public schools to introduce such manual courses as sewing; and in his larger view he saw the curriculum as contributing to industrial development on a nationwide scale. "The need for Hampton's work seems to increase every year, and we are endeavoring to extend the school's influence by developing and carrying out General Armstrong's plan of giving these people a practical, industrial education which shall fit them to go out into the south and the west and help their people."[13]

Along with training teachers who would go out into the South and teach others, Frissell was deeply committed to re-

ligious training and character building. He states this
philosophy to Mrs. R. H. Adams of Radford, Virginia: "It is our
purpose that all the influences brought to bear upon these
students at their work as well as in the classrooms, shall always
tend to improve and strengthen their character."[14]

He defended his position of giving manual training to
students and made a commitment to teaching as one of the requirements for admittance to the institution. Such training was
more important than a "classical" education.

We do not at all disparage classical education at Hampton, for we
know its value, and believe that a certain number of the youth of the
colored race should receive a classical education; but the great question before the race at the present time is how they are to obtain
decent homes, how are they to clothe themselves, and how are they to
obtain sufficient property so that they shall be able to hold their own
with members of the white race. Our aim now is to send out into the
country districts of the south, young people who shall not only be
teachers in the schools, but also those who can cultivate the land, start
shops, and present an object lesson to their people of industrious,
decent Christian living.[15]

He expressed this view even more emphatically to H. L. Wayland: "I do not feel that the colored man because of his color
ought to be shut out from Latin and Greek. But the average
colored man, like the average white man, needs many other
things more than Caesar's Commentaries."[16]

In letters thanking patrons for their contributions and asking
them to support his ideas for new programs and projects, he
outlined many of his innovations. On the very practical level
they included a cooking school: "As we are anxious to get the
cooking department started, I have engaged a teacher from
New York."[17] On the level of curriculum development, it included attention to very young students: "We are anxious to obtain an instructor in kindergarten work, who will not only be
able to teach children, but can also give instruction to those who
are themselves to be teachers."[18] And, in keeping with his idea
of mission, Frissell thought that "Hampton should be the training ground for colored kindergartens in the south."[19] He
constantly sought to reach beyond the confines of the campus

to influence and to help the general community. One such project for which he solicited sponsorship was a traveling library: "We are starting out traveling libraries among our graduates who are teaching in the country schools of the South, and I think the books you sent will be of great help along these lines."[20]

Frissell felt that once the students had completed their education, they had an obligation to go out and teach. He took note that the public schools in the South were inadequate, and he wrote letters, talked with the leaders of the country, and held summer workshops to try to improve the educational system. His letters indicate his concern and understanding, and he offered some solutions to the many educational problems. This included, of course, the influence of Hampton's graduates. "In response I would say that while great stress in our work has been laid upon sending out men and women who shall uplift the masses of their people in the south, there are occasionally those who go out to work in the north."[21] But even more teachers would be sent to the South: "Our thought on the matter . . . is to prepare teachers of dressmaking, sewing, cooking, and laundering, who shall be able to teach in the south in connection with the public schools and other institutions."[22] In Frissell's view, the Hampton graduates would also press for related reforms. "I feel very strongly the importance of pressing this work as it concerns the general subject of education in the south. . . . I saw a number of white gentlemen and found their feeling in favor of industrial education for both whites and blacks, is very strong—also there is a need to lengthen the school term."[23] One of the reforms he urged was lengthening the public school term so that students entering Hampton would be better prepared. Further, Frissell says, such reform occasionally required agitation. "Our advanced Normal Department opened successfully with some eight pupils. Two of whom have come as graduates of high schools from the North. . . . Already one of our graduates has been sent out with the definite purpose of stirring up the colored people to demand longer school terms and better teachers."[24] Frissell was not hesitant about committing Hampton's resources to encourage educational reform: "There is a great lack of superintendence of schools all through the south." He sent out G. S. Dickerman to "stir up the colored people to increase the school term," showing his faith in the people he was serving.[25]

He also showed complete trust in his students and continued to write about them at every opportunity. The following letter illustrates both his respect and his expectations:

I feel . . . that you ought to understand that we can not make any strict rules for our students here. They are earnest young people who have come out from hard conditions, and in many cases bad conditions, but have cast them aside, and have such a thorough knowledge of their bad effects, that we are able to trust them and do trust them. . . .

The boys and girls meet in the dining room and have social intercourse. Of course their quarters are not separated, and yet it would be very easy for anyone who had not strength to withstand temptation to escape. . . . if it seems that she needs more than ordinary supervision or shows indications of a lack of moral character, we would not keep her.[26]

To the secretary of the Pennsylvania Society to Protect Children from Cruelty, he described Hampton's disciplinary procedures: "We have not been accustomed to employ corporal punishment at Hampton, but we are unwilling to say that we would not make use of it under certain circumstances. In certain cases of displin [sic] boys are placed in a lock-up usually with little variation in diet."[27]

Frissell devoted the majority of his efforts toward raising the money necessary to insure that Hampton Institute would have a secure future with expanded vocational, industrial, and academic programs to offer a quality education to all of its students. After he was highly successful in these efforts, he moved on to the curriculum. He also pressed for a more adequate education for all of the children in the South. But in addition to expressing his views in letters, he published books and many articles in the *Southern Workman,* a journal which he vigorously supported. "We are anxious to make the *Southern Workman* the medium of communication with the colored people all over the south."[28]

True to his training, however, he further expounded his

ideas in speeches and sermons, such as the Baccalaureate sermon in 1890 in which he exhorted his students to continue the work begun by Hampton:

These school days have been to you the entrance into the promised land, into higher thoughts, loftier aspirations, clearer views of life. You can never go back into the life of Egypt and the wilderness. Remember that you are to reach forward to those things that are before. Do not be satisfied with your present attainments in knowledge. Be students wherever you are, students of God's word, students of nature and of men. Reach forward to higher attainments in character, greater strength to resist temptations, greater purity of thought and life, more love for others. . . .

In an especial sense you, the educated young men and women of these races, have a high and holy calling. In an especial sense you are called to be kings and priests to your people. You have the power to mould and shape them as those that come after you cannot do. You, with God's help, can bring to them "the new heavens and the new earth wherein dwelleth righteousness."[29]

Frissell made passionate pleas for the support of his work in Negro education. One of the best examples of his oratory, undoubtedly influenced by his training for the ministry, is his speech to the National Education Association in 1916. After quoting a story about a mountain climber who saved himself by cutting the rope on two men hanging below him, Frissell urged, with full paternalistic drama, that "blacks are the disinherited children. Don't cut the rope."[30]

Notes

1. To C. B. Pope, Chicago, Ill., Nov. 30, 1894, Hollis B. Frissell Papers, Archives, Hampton Institute, Hampton, Va. All subsequent letters cited are in the Frissell Papers.

2. To I. Garland Penn, Lynchburg, Va., Dec. 10, 1894.

3. To M. A. Butt, Bay, N.C., Sept. 9, 1895.

4. To Mrs. George Ladd, New Haven, Conn., Oct. 28, 1896.

5. To the Reverend Samuel Macauley Jackson, New York, N.Y., May 15, 1896.

6. To John S. Barnes, New York, N.Y., Jan. 29, 1897.

7. To Jacob Naylor, Hotel Walton, Philadelphia, Pa., Feb. 1898.

8. "A Binder of Sections," *Southern Workman* 46 (1917), 571.

9. F. G. Peabody, *Education for Life: The Story of Hampton Institute* (Garden City, N.Y.: Doubleday, Page and Co., 1926), pp. 227– 41.

10. To C. Cope, Philadelphia, Pa., Oct. 31, 1895.

11. To J. J. McWilliams, Buffalo, N.Y., May 25, 1896.

12. To Mrs. Mary F. Merwin, Brooklyn, N.Y.,Nov. 15, 1897.

13. To William Endicott, Boston, Mass., Feb. 8, 1898.

14. To Mrs. R. H. Adams, Radford, Va., Oct. 26, 1895.

15. To Professor F. G. Smith, Nashville, Tenn., Feb. 16, 1897.

16. To the Reverend H. L. Wayland, D.D., Philadelphia, Pa., May 16, 1895.

17. To Miss A. M. Horman, Boston Normal School of Gymnastics, Boston, Mass., Oct. 20, 1896.

18. To Professor Clarence F. Carroll, Worcester, Mass., Apr. 29, 1898.

19. To Miss M. P. Trask, Cambridge, Md., June 4, 1898.

20. To Miss Fannie J. Beebe, New Haven, Conn., Oct. 20, 1896.

21. To Mrs. M. F. Morse, Rosell, N.J., Jan. 14, 1898.

22. To Mrs. P. W. Sprague, Charlestown, Mass., Jan. 17, 1898.

23. To Robert Ogden, Philadelphia, Pa., Mar. 17, 1899.

24. To J. L. M. Curry, Washington, D.C., Nov. 4, 1897.

25. To George Foster Peabody, New York, N.Y., Mar. 17, 1899.

26. To Mrs. Sarah Dickinson, Middlefield, Conn., Nov. 4, 1897.

27. To J. L. Crew, Philadelphia, Pa., Oct. 1, 1896.

28. To George Inge, Charlottesville, Va., Nov. 13, 1897.

29. Frissell, "Finished; Yet Just Begun," Baccalaureate Sermon, May 19, 1890, pp. 12– 13, Frissell Papers, Archives, Hampton Institute.

30. Frissell, "The Education of the Negro," *Addresses and Proceedings of the Fifty-fourth Annual Meeting,* National Education Association, vol. 54 (1916), p. 111.

Portraits in Black: Illustrated Poems of Paul Laurence Dunbar
Nancy B. McGhee

> And so thou'rt gone, O brother to the night!
> After the years of waiting and the pain,
> After the striving and the stress thou'rt gone!
>
> .   .   .   .   .
>
> And when in some far-off hereafter day
> The voice of Fame shall speak her last decree
> When she shall summon from the wreck of worlds
> The names that Time's great movement shall defeat
> And when then she shall stand beside thy tomb,
> The laurel in her hand, and think on thee,
> Tis then will be thy word upon the scroll:
> *He voiced the yearning of a people's soul.*[1]

WITH THESE WORDS Benjamin Brawley—teacher, scholar and critic—added his eulogy to the chorus of praise and lament that arose upon the death of Paul Laurence Dunbar in 1906. For those who knew him personally, "the poet and his song" were now silenced in death; but for all the millions who were to share the beauty of his "song" through the delights, humor, and fancy of his verse, Paul Dunbar was to live in the memories of famous writers—James Whitcomb Riley, Eugene Field, James Weldon Johnson, Benjamin Brawley—and in the illustrated photographs that accompanied six volumes of his published poems.

The editorials and essays that flooded the literary scene in commemoration of his unique contribution as the first Black professional poet in themselves reflect the variety of personalities to whom his poetry brought delight and entertainment. Foremost among his contemporaries who offered tributes to the poet were Mary Church Terrell, W. S. Scarborough, president of Wilberforce University, and one of the editors of the *Southern Workman*, who recalled that "Mr.

Dunbar was boyish in appearance, modest and unaffected in demeanor, and when reciting his verses showed dramatic power, as well as humor, tenderness, and sentiment"[2] Lida Keck Wiggins, whose *Life and Works of Paul Laurence Dunbar* has provided basic materials for numerous studies of the poet, supports this view of Dunbar's personableness in the section of her work labeled "A Series of Personal Reminiscences."

A characteristic that appealed particularly to me was his impulsive way of showing delight when I chanced to mention the name of some one who proved to be a common friend.

After we had conversed for possibly an hour Mr. Dunbar reminded Miss May that she had not yet "read" for him. As her cultured voice gave utterance to the lines of several of his favorite selections it was interesting to study the changing expressions upon the poet's face. At one point he laughed aloud almost boisterously, at another he was moved to tears. In every line of his fine face one could see the evidence of culture and the shining of the poetic mind.

Impressed by the easy and pleasant manner of the famous poet during her visit, Mrs. Wiggins commented, "Modesty concerning his work and the great honors it has brought him are marked characteristics of the poet."[3] To his friends Paul Laurence Dunbar became a symbol of kindness, gentility, and talent. In "Some Personal Reminiscences of Paul Laurence Dunbar," Edward F. Arnold later agreed with William Dean Howells that "Paul Laurence Dunbar was the only man of pure African blood and of American civilization to feel the Negro life aesthetically and to express it lyrically; and that a race which had come to this effect in any member of it, had attained civilization in him. His poem 'Ere Sleep Comes Down to Soothe the Weary Eyes' is a production worthy of the greatest."[4]

By the time of his death the romantic story of Paul Laurence Dunbar had been established by myth and legend, by controversy and criticism, by fact and fiction that together made him a hero among Blacks in America. In the decade before his death the literary career of Dunbar had progressed rapidly, with recognition and praise coming from the great of the land. For the thousands of Dunbar admirers, the "dark youth, singing in the dawn of a new freedom," had become the symbol of the artistic and intellectual potential of Black folk. The poet's blossoming achievements, interrupted before the peak by his untimely death, evoked excesses of praise, recollections, and critical evaluations. In the short span of one decade—from the publication of *Lyrics of Lowly Life* (1896) to *Joggin' Erlong* (1906)—Paul Dunbar looked into the smiling face of fame and also suffered inexpressibly the pains of his frail body intermingled with the weaknesses, sorrows, and depression of the human spirit.

At the age of twenty-four, after severe struggles with poverty during which doubts and misfortunes were assuaged by the faith and assistance of a few loyal friends, this talented young writer was on his way to national acclaim. But not without problems. Now that the great critic William Dean Howells had publicly praised his works and had written the introduction to *Lyrics of Lowly Life*, national recognition would be forthcoming. Yet racism in America was a constant menace, then as now, widely accepted by many but bitterly resented and often opposed. That the talented poet of his predominantly white high school class in Dayton, Ohio, could find work only as an elevator boy testifies to the tactic of keeping the Black man in his place. The discovery of the economic strictures placed upon the Black man by American society was extremely disheartening to young Dunbar, who was then and later the sole support of his mother. More painful to him was his observation of the obvious economic success and advancement of his former schoolmates and friends Orville and Wilbur Wright. When he visited their bicycle shop, he saw the promise of success open to white men who possessed talent, responsibility, and vision. Yet at the age of twenty Dunbar looked to the future with hope, enthusiasm, and idealism.

The 1890s were years of choice and challenge, of progress and defeat in the social and political life of America. To some this decade became the Gay Nineties, decked in the glitter of the Gilded Age. To others, those politically oriented, the 1890s signaled the rise of American imperialism, as they viewed the new expansionism into Hawaii, the imposition of the Monroe Doctrine, the Cuban crisis, the Spanish-American War.[5] To the Black man 1890 marked the end of Reconstruction, leaving

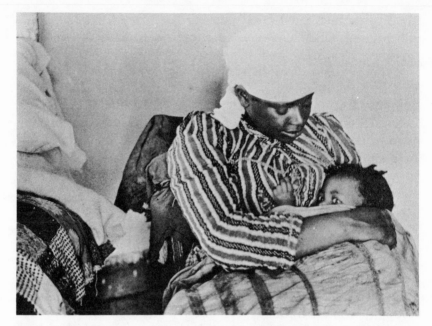

Illustration for Paul Laurence Dunbar's "Long To'ds Night" in *When Malindy Sings*

him bound by economic slavery and encased in a society which stripped him of his vote and thereby deprived him of political power. In the nineties Jim Crow was becoming a firmly established way of life. C. Vann Woodward has delineated the basic philosophy of the era as it affected the foundation of American democracy: "All the defenses of Negro voting crumbled in the latter part of the nineteenth century. . . . Ingenious ways of making voting difficult or embarrassing for Negroes were devised. The Negro vote was diminished a great deal before formal disenfranchisement took place. But between 1890–1910, with the approbation of the Supreme Court, disenfranchisement was made virtually complete."[6]

A specific example of the political situation faced by Blacks following the compromise of 1877 is related in the following account: "On election day thousands of terrified Negroes were hiding in the swamps or staying in their cabins. In some places the only Negroes who could vote were those who showed Democratic ballots or who were accompanied to the polls by white men. Many who were bold enough to carry Republican ballots were fired upon or driven from the polls."[7]

As the 1890s passed into history, the prospect of participation by Black men and women in American political, economic, and social advancement grew more bleak. There is therefore little wonder that differing responses to the situation came from Frederick Douglass, Booker T. Washington, and W. E. B. Du Bois. On the other hand, there were a few whites who loved justice and mercy—and walked humbly with their God. One of these, novelist Albion Tourgee, at the Lake Mohonk Conference, June 4–6, 1890, stated:

So far as the peaceful and Christian solution of the race problem is concerned, indeed, I am inclined to think that the only education required is that of the *white* race. The hate, the oppression, the injustice, are all on our side; and every Negro who wins the honors of his class in a Northern college, becomes a cashier in a national bank in Topeka, writes a story which New England people read, publishes a newspaper which white people are compelled to peruse, wins a membership in the Boston Press Club . . . or so good a ball-player that a crack club has to secure his services lest another should—each and every one of these colored men is a missionary sent of God to the white people of the United States, to teach them the fundamental truth of Christianity.[8]

Basically, the role of Blacks was the same throughout the land. Just as Richard Wright was forced to learn "the ethics of living Jim Crow" nearly a half-century later, so also was Dunbar required to learn and endure the unhappy fact of being Black in America in 1891.

The parents of Dunbar had seen the harsh realities of life in bondage in the South and had rebelled in their individual ways. Each of them had passed through the tension-filled days of Reconstruction and had survived the tightening noose of prejudice and repression until they felt desperate enough to move. Joshua and Matilda Dunbar made their way to the North, where their son Paul was born into a world relatively "free." In Dayton, Ohio, Matilda Dunbar regaled her young son with stories of slavery narrated without bitterness and sorrow. She focused her tales on the pleasantries and incidents—human-

Illustration for Paul Laurence Dunbar's "Time to Tinker 'Roun' " in *Poems of Cabin and Field*

interest accounts. Her insights were so penetrating that these tales became a reservoir of situations and characters that stimulated the lively creativity and imagination of her talented son. Characterized by brilliant and lively wit, Dunbar's short stories, such as "Jim's Probation" and "Anner 'Lizer's Stumblin' Block," present an inside view of plantation life blending realism, irony, and humor with a knowledgeableness that suggests the author's direct contact with the scene and the incidents. In his poetry Dunbar not only revealed these qualities but also sought excellence in form and style. In a recent discussion of Dunbar, Professor Darwin Turner offers convincing argument that "Dunbar, seeking distinction as a poet, consciously and extensively experimented with meter and rhyme throughout his career. Even in his first major volume, *Lyrics of Lowly Life* (1896), Dunbar consciously studied and experimented with forms, metrical patterns and rhyme schemes."[9]

Lyrics of Lowly Life, resulting from five years of struggle against poverty, became a landmark on the stony road to success. This book carried the influential Introduction written by William Dean Howells, which has stimulated much discussion by critics of Dunbar.[10] It was here that the dialect poems were intermingled with the poems in Standard English and were highlighted by the attention given them by Howells, who conceived the significant feature of *Lyrics of Lowly Life* to be that "here was the first instance of an American negro who had evidenced innate distinction in literature."[11]

Addison Gayle and other modern Black critics take issue with Howells, pointing out that there were Black poets before Dunbar who wrote dialect poetry as well as poetry in Standard English. Gayle characterizes Howells's judgment as a combination of insult and praise. Most of the critics, however, seem to agree with Benjamin Brawley that in *Lyrics of Lowly Life* Dunbar had "found himself." But Brawley had some reservations about *Lyrics of Lowly Life:*

As a piece of book-making, *Majors and Minors* was not as good as *Oak and Ivy.* The paper was thinner and duller, and the selection and arrangement of type was not quite so admirable. . . . At the same time, if we consider only original work, that is, the number of excellent pieces that had not previously appeared in a book, *Majors and Minors becomes the most notable collection of poems ever issued by a Negro in the United States.* The next volume, *Lyrics of Lowly Life,* was in better form and, having a standard publisher, must ultimately be regarded as more important; but most of what was good in that book had already appeared in *Majors and Minors.* [12]

Nevertheless, the success of *Lyrics of Lowly Life* gave the initial boost to the fame and national acclaim that characterized Dunbar's achievement during the next ten years of his life. The popularity of certain poems, such as "Ere Sleep Comes Down to Soothe the Weary Eyes," with which the collection opened, and "The Party," with which it closed, heralded the thousands of readings and recitations among a people who were proud that Paul Laurence Dunbar was indeed and in fact a Black man, descended directly from African slaves.

Three years and numerous poems, stories, and a novel later, Dunbar published his first illustrated collection of poems, *Poems of Cabin and Field* (1899). Dunbar described these years as the "pouring time" because so many opportunities came to him. [13] In addition to his publications and readings, he toured England enjoying many exhilarating and rewarding experiences, meeting old friends such as Hallie Q. Brown, but also suffering economic misfortune from which he was rescued by his faithful friends, among them Dr. Alexander Crummel and Dr. H. A. Tobey. Dunbar had become a national figure and was busily writing and making appearances reciting his poems. A job at the Library of Congress, for which a friend recommended him, gave him an opportunity to settle in Washington, D.C., where his circle of associates included many of the Negro leaders of the day. He had previously gained the friendship of Frederick Douglass during the early days of struggle in Chicago. Now among the established leaders he claimed the friendship of Kelly Miller, Mary Church Terrell, and other well-known personalities of his race living in Washington. Among his contemporaries in the arts, he associated continuously with the Johnson brothers, J. Rosamond and James Weldon. Will Marion Cook, Bert Williams, Ford Dabney, Harry Burleigh, Sr., and other musical artists who gathered at the Marshall Hotel in New York also became his friends.

Dunbar was also making his poems known through readings at Black colleges, such as Howard University, Tuskegee Institute, and Hampton Institute. Several letters written by Principal Hollis B. Frissell of Hampton Institute and addressed to "Mr. Paul Laurence Dunbar at Congressional Library, Washington, D.C.," confirm the opinion that a cordial relationship between the administration of the Virginia school and the young author was developing as early as 1898. On December 24, 1897, Principal Frissell wrote to the poet:

Our Armstrong Association in New York has engaged the Astor Gallery for a meeting on the 13th of February, Monday afternoon. We shall be glad to pay you fifty dollars for your services on that afternoon. As far as I know the hour of the meeting has not been arranged, but I presume that it will be three o'clock as last year.

I should like very much to have you come to Hampton whenever you can, but as I do not feel that we can pay you the amount for a reading that you usually obtain, and as I do not like to ask you to come without it, I fear that we shall be deprived of the pleasure of seeing you. Miss Bacon has, I think, already written you asking for some contribution for "The Southern Workman."

Kindly let me know as soon as convenient in regard to the New York meeting as we shall have to make some other arrangement if you can not come.[14]

Apparently the invitation was accepted, for it appears that the letters of Frissell and Dunbar crossed in the mail. On December 29, 1897, the principal replied:

Your kind letter of the 23rd is at hand and we shall expect you for the afternoon of February 13th. I think that the story was altogether satisfactory, though perhaps Miss Bacon would rather it had reference to colored rather than white people, but that is not of very great importance.

I hope you will realize that you will always be a welcome guest whenever it may suit your convenience to come to us.[15]

The reference to "the story" is very likely to Dunbar's "A Southern Silhouette," a short story that appeared in the *Southern Workman* in January 1899.

Further explanation of the plans for the Armstrong meeting in New York appear in Frissell's letter of January 10, 1898:

I am glad to know from your card of the 8th that you are likely to be at the meeting in New York on the afternoon of February 11th. I have not myself yet heard the details of the meeting, but the plan was to have an author's reading at which Mr. John Kendrick Bangs is to preside, and then Hopkinson Smith and Mrs. Ruth McEnery Stuart and others whose names I do not know, have promised to take part.

The meeting will be under the general care of the Armstrong Association of New York, of which Dr. William Schieffelin is president. The first thought in regard to it was to have it a reading for colored authors entirely, but after consideration it seemed to me wiser to make it more general. I hope very much that you will be able to be present for my thought was that it would be well to give some prominence to what has been done in literature by members of the colored race.

Please remember that we should at any time be pleased to see you here at Hampton, and you may always be sure of a very cordial welcome. I should be glad to have the School meet you and know you, for we are very proud of what you have accomplished.

I called to see you on Saturday of last week, but was not able to get at you.[16]

It is evident that the arrangement for this meeting involved several well-known personalities and that the Hampton Institute principal was unable to be present. Yet he had personally arranged for the fee to be paid to the poet to avoid inconvenience, according to his letter of February 6, 1898, referring to the $50 to be paid to Dunbar in New York, and requesting that the poet occupy "considerable time" in the reading of poems, and "possibly" some of the prose writings.

The *Southern Workman* described the meeting at the Waldorf as an occasion planned "for the benefit of Hampton Institute" and promised that Mr. Dunbar would read "some of his *Lyrics of Lowly Life*." As an added attraction, the article announced that "the Hampton Quartette will sing plantation melodies and an Indian boy from Hampton will give an account of the Indian Medicine Man." Other southern authors of note were expected to appear, including the popular writer Mrs. Ruth McEnery Stuart, who would read selections from her own short stories. In a later letter to the poet, Principal Frissell, exhibiting his usual active interest in the literary and artistic life of Hampton Institute, requested Mr. Dunbar to become a regular contribu-

tor to the *Southern Workman,* along with numerous other rising
young literary artists and outstanding community leaders.[17]

In accepting the invitation to contribute to this periodical,
Dunbar joined a growing number of local and national authors
who reflected the hopes, aspirations, and ambitions of Black
people whose lives and labors took place in the Atlantic Sea-
board states. Although the earlier issues of the periodical
sought to implement its devotion to the "working classes of the
South," through its pages moved an impressive procession of
personalities in the arts, religion, and education. In every issue
of the *Southern Workman* appeared accounts of meetings,
concerts, art shows, and articles ranging from news of
Hampton graduates in Africa to the debates regarding Indian
education at Hampton. Alumni of "the Hampton School" sent
back to their alma mater reports of their struggles, their suc-
cesses, and sometimes their failures as they worked in the rural
communities of Virginia, North Carolina, Florida, and
Georgia. In turn, they read of the events on the campus of "the
Normal School," such as the musical and cultural concerts and
activities that abounded on that busy campus. The major visitors who lectured and met with the students, as Dunbar was
later to do, reflected the intellectual and religious interests of
the Black workers—teachers and artisans, preachers and
laymen, local alumni and friends. The humor and pathos of the
Dunbar poems and short stories embellished the color and
luster of the *Southern Workman,* in which most of his works from
1899 to 1906 were reviewed and many of them were published.

The vitality and vigor of the poems that flowed from the pen
of Paul Laurence Dunbar between 1898 and 1906, when he
died, offered his readers homely, humorous, entertaining
scenes and provided characterizations that were unique
portraits of typical members of the Black community at this
time. The realities of existence for Black men and women,
young and old, were harsh and rugged at the turn of the
century.[18] When a poet such as Dunbar gleaned from the daily
activities of "lowly life" the pleasant scenes of young love, or
parental affection, or the joys of childhood, then his reader
could see, feel, hear, and understand the poetry of daily
existence. Because of his descriptive and imaginative powers,

Paul Dunbar's poems were especially suited for the popular collections of illustrated volumes, published with decorations in the manner of the late 1890s and the early 1900s. Six of the seven illustrated volumes of Dunbar poems owe their illustrations and decorations to the interest, imagination, and artistic talents of approximately twenty members of the faculty and staff of Hampton Institute.

The minutes of the Kiquotan Kamera Klub dated October 21, 1893, read: "A party of Hampton teachers met in Room 21, Science Building on the evening of October 21, 1893, for the purpose of organizing a Camera Club. Mr. Brown called the meeting to order and presided until Mr. Turner was elected President. Mr. Brown and Miss Davis were appointed a committee to suggest a name for the club at the next meeting, and Mr. Turner, Mr. Briggs and Mrs. Armstrong, a committee to formulate a constitution or statement of the club's aim and regulation."[19] With this meeting the camera club began its artistic life, which continued until November 22, 1926. For the first year, Miss L. E. Herron, who contributed many years of service to the library of Hampton Institute, became the secretary. The name Kiquotan Kamera Klub was inserted in the next minutes (October 27, 1893) and other provisions and articles were approved:

II. The object of this society is the cultivation and promotion of photography.
III. All persons interested in photography as amateurs are eligible to [sic] membership.
IV. All members shall be entitled to free use of the library, dark room, etc. and to take part in all meetings and discussions.
V.   The annual fee for members shall be one dollar on joining the society, and at the end of each following twelve months.
VI. Each member shall be expected to bring in some work each month for benefit of the club. Failure for three successive months shall forfeit membership unless excused by the club.[20]

The officers, their duties, and other regulations being listed, the constitution made provision for changes and modifications as needed in the future. The signatories of this initial group included members of the faculty at Hampton Institute whose names are well known: Lenora E. Herron, R. R. Moton, J. E. Davis, M. A. Armstrong, H. W. Howe, H. B. Turner, J. B. Frissell. Between 1893 and 1899 the Kiquotan Kamera Klub witnessed times of prosperity, gaiety, relaxation as well as occasions of depression when the membership dropped or interest flagged. The members were kept busy seeking and maintaining equipment, securing acceptable places to hold meetings, and selecting poems they could illustrate effectively and attractively.

Coincidentally, 1893 was a very significant year in the poetic career of Paul Laurence Dunbar from the viewpoint of contacts and friendships; the period in Chicago broadened his horizons. It has been suggested that he may have met George Washington Carver, not at that time a scientist, but a young man whose painting *Yucca Glorioso* had won honorable mention among the state's exhibitions.[21] It is also interesting that during the Chicago period Dunbar met the feminists Ida B. Wells, Hallie Q. Brown, and Mary Church Terrell, with whom he later had a close association as friend and neighbor in Washington. Terrell's high regard for the poet is seen in her tribute to him following his death, when she referred to the several days spent with him and his mother in Dayton approximately a year before he died:

I account it a privilege to have had such an excellent opportunity of becoming acquainted with the greatest poet the race has ever produced. . . . I discovered there were depths in the character that I had never sounded and qualities of heart of which I had never dreamed, although I saw him frequently when he lived in Washington.

. . . I shall always think of his patience under his severe affliction as a veritable miracle of modern times.

. . . The weakness and inertia of his worn and wasted body contrasted sadly and strangely with the strength and activity of his vigorous mind. . . .

Personally I believe he will occupy as high a place in American literature as Burns in the British, if not higher.[22]

This period of early productivity for Dunbar may be seen as "seed time" also for the Kiquotan Kamera Klub. The amateur photographers had made advances in the techniques of picture taking and developing prints. On campus the club had acquired and decorated a room in the Science Building and had made considerable progress in studying and selecting provocative subjects for their pictures. For example, in October 1895 the group approved the suggestion of Miss Davis, who recommended that "a poem be illustrated with each member deciding what illustration he or she would take."[23] At this meeting Miss Herron suggested that "after learning to use the lantern slides the members have the poem read at the close of the year with the illustrations." Apparently this idea became the basic activity of the club in establishing the whole concept of illustration of poems and other literary pieces.

In America the practice of illustrating books had been used by some publishers since colonial times, but according to one student of the matter, "no single aspect of book production in the U.S. has been more consistently neglected by students than the illustration of books in the period before 1860."[24] The history of American bookmaking includes wood engraving and the later technical refinements thereof. It appears that Harper encouraged artists and engravers during the mid-century, publishing the Bible of 1843 and illustrating it with approximately eighteen hundred wood engravings. In 1871 Harper was producing "lively and natural illustrations, somewhat uneven in artistic quality" as in David Hunter Strother's *Virginia Illustrated.* The idea of visually representing the scenes depicted in a poem or story seemed to be catching on in American book publishing as techniques became more sophisticated. By the time of the poetic achievements of Paul Laurence Dunbar, book illustrating by photography had become a rewarding pastime for amateurs such as those who belonged to the Kiquotan Kamera Klub. These educators realized that "genuine illustrations, in the best sense of the word, are E. W. Kemble's pictures for Mark Twain's *Huckleberry Finn.* Once you have read an edition with his illustrations, you will continue to see the people and the scenes of this book as Kemble saw them."

There is little doubt that teachers at Hampton had read Keats's poems illustrated by Will H. Low, published in 1885 and 1886, as well as the edition of Rossetti's *Blessed Damozel,* illustrated by Kenyon Cox, 1886. These popular English poets were widely read in America during the mid-nineteenth century. For example, the handwritten edition of the *Rubaiyat* (1884) was "so full of ornamental allusions and hidden symbols, that the decorations have to be explained in detail at the end of the volume."[25] They might even have seen Dunbar's "A Coquette Conquered" from *Lyrics of Lowly Life* (1896), reprinted in the *Century* with a sketch illustration by Peter Newell, "the first published illustration for a Dunbar poem."[26]

During the period of incubation between examining illustrated editions and actually producing their own, the enthusiastic members of the Kiquotan Kamera Klub were at work developing and refining their photographic skills. They produced three albums of blue prints which, according to Eleanor Gilman, assistant to the director of the Hampton Archives, depicted scenes "of the campus, and boats . . . on Hampton Creek and the neighboring Hampton Roads."[27] Among the interesting and financially productive activities of the club was the annual twelve-page calendar presenting historical scenes on campus. This calendar was circulated throughout the United States and received much commendation. Frequently the exhibitions of photographs taken by members brought the peninsula community to the campus for a kind of open house or community cultural occasion. Critiques in the local press pointed out the progress made by the members who won prizes and honors for their choice of subject as well as for their photographic skills.

Then, against this background suggesting normal club procedure, the minutes of October 29, 1897, and January 28, 1898, record that "Paul Laurence Dunbar's poem, 'The Deserted Plantation,' was suggested for illustrating, and members were requested to bring in negatives at the next meeting. . . . [January 29] . . . Negatives and prints for illustrating 'The Deserted Plantation' were brought in and examined and the poem read. Many of the negatives were found desirable, and others were to be brought in at the next meeting." That the club was particularly interested in a Dunbar poem is clear because further illustrations of "The Deserted Plantation" were accepted and a committee composed of Mr. Riley (to whom went an award for first prize in competitions), Miss Davis, and Miss Proctor was appointed to judge the productions. At the regular club meeting in May 1898 the minutes offer the following information:

> The subject for the illustrations for "The Deserted Plantation" was discussed and the committee reported that only five or six of the illustrations were lacking. It was suggested that if the illustrations are satisfactory Mr. Turner submit the collection of the club to Dodd and Mead, in N.Y. . . .
>
> It was voted that a meeting be held as late as the presence of the members allowed, and that a copy of the lines still requiring illustration be given to each member of the club by the Librarian. It was decided that the subject for work should be the frontispiece for "The Deserted Plantation" to be handed in accompanied by a negative in some other line. The price was left to be determined at the next meeting. . . .
>
> Fourteen negatives were handed in at this meeting. The prize was awarded to Mrs. Armstrong for her picture of Dan.

With this exchange of ideas at the club meeting the story of the Kiquotan Kamera Klub and its study of Dunbar's poetry began. Evidently, the procedure of the club had become fairly clear:

1. Each member was expected to produce a minimum number of photographs.

2. Each member was responsible for interpretive illustration of designated poems or lines from poems or other literary works.

3. Samples of the club's work at the April 15, 1898, Exhibition indicate that the members sought to penetrate "every field of amateur work . . . through out-door photography, both landscape and Marine dominated."[28]

In the fall term of 1898 the Kiquotan Kamera Klub had not only acquired for itself the acclaim registered by the local press, but was also planning to illustrate a group of poems written by Paul Laurence Dunbar and published by Dodd, Mead and Company. A letter from the publisher, read at a special club meeting on January 21, 1899, proposed that the club expand its commitment beyond illustrations of the one poem, "The

Deserted Plantation," for which club members had made illustrations, to the preparation of a set of illustrations for a small
volume of selected poems, later entitled *Poems of Cabin and
Field*. In February 1899 the club met again in Griggs Hall and
learned that the firm now offered $150 instead of $100. There
were to be fifty pictures to be ready by the middle of June. Selections from photographs already submitted for "The
Deserted Plantation" had been made by the publisher, and
those not used would be returned to the club for possible use in
the illustration of other poems. The club studied the poems
and voted to undertake the work, asking the same committee
which collected illustrations for "The Deserted Plantation" to
serve for the larger assignment. Members expressed concern
about limitation of time and about selection of poems to be
illustrated, and the club went on record as "wishing to add
'Christmas is Coming,' found in the December issue of the
Bookman." Attention was drawn also to the fact that the $100 of-
fered by the publisher was a small compensation (even at that
time) for the number of pictures and the amount of work required.[29]

In the meantime H. B. Turner, the first president of the club
and chaplain at Hampton Institute, called upon Dodd, Mead
and Company, who received him well. The publishers seemed
"very much pleased with the quality and appropriateness of the
photographs already submitted and very glad that the
Hampton club had undertaken the work."

The rather involved process of reading and studying poems,
conceiving and planning appropriate illustrations, and
persuading reluctant subjects to participate in the project was a
time-consuming endeavor. Persons who posed for the
photographs would need to be contacted, the purpose of the
photographer precisely explained, and a time set for the pic-
ture-taking exercise. Patience, diplomacy, and a high degree
of dedication must have abounded among club members to
achieve the results desired by author, publisher, photographer,
and screening committee. The Dunbar poems so optimistically
and enthusiastically accepted by the club upon Turner's report
following his visit in New York were only eight in number; yet
whatever may be the present-day assessment of their literary

Illustration for Paul Laurence Dunbar's "A Banjo Song" in *Poems of Cabin and Field*

quality, the fact is that these poems possessed the power of seizing the imagination and emotions of approximately twenty staff members of the Hampton school.

At the turn of the century the artistic and literary tastes of sensitive readers were certainly very different from those that prevailed during the Harlem Renaissance two decades later, when World War I helped set in motion the great migration of Blacks from the rural South to the urban North. Written in what critics recognize as the plantation tradition, nurtured by Joel Chandler Harris and Thomas Nelson Page, *Poems of Cabin and Field* reflects general attitudes expressed in the following statement from the *Southern Workman* of June 1899:

The Camera Club is pushing to completion its work of illustrating Mr. Dunbar's poems for the publishers, Messrs. Dodd, Mead & Co. of New York. There are eight of these poems, most of which have already appeared elsewhere . . . with about fifty illustrations from negatives which the club is making for this purpose.

This club has been in existence among the teachers here for several years, and has made a more or less valuable collection of pictures of the school and its surroundings, including many studies of Negro cabins. . . . But the study of the old-time life of coloured people which is involved in these illustrations is by far the most interesting if not valuable work which it has undertaken. . . .

The poems themselves are wonderfully true in their descriptions of a life which is rapidly passing away.[30]

In what manner was the camera club busily "pushing to completion" this task? After the members read and studied the poems selected for illustration, they finally decided that each member of the club should undertake what he or she pleased — and efforts for special pictures should be made later.[31] The eight poems chosen for the first venture by author, publisher, and club engaged in this unique project are (from the table of contents of the 1899 *Poems of Cabin and Field*) as follows:

1. "The Deserted Plantation"
2. "Hunting Song"
3. "Little Brown Baby"
4. "Chris'mus is a-Comin' "
5. "Signs of the Times"

6. "Time to Tinker 'Round"
7. "Lullaby"
8. "A Banjo Song"

Interestingly enough, this is not the order of arrangement which the club suggested.[32]

At this point a number of elements and characteristics of the situation with respect to illustrating the Dunbar poems may be established. First, Paul Laurence Dunbar was known throughout the nation, and despite the controversy over the use of dialect in literature — a controversy yet to be settled — the growing popularity of the poet made the publication of favorite Dunbar poems a significant event. Second, with the rising interest in photography as a means of book illustration, in many instances replacing the woodcut, sooner or later a camera club such as that at Hampton Institute would perceive interesting pictorial elements in the vivid imagery of Dunbar. Although the old way of life was fading from the Hampton community at the turn of the century, the illustrations for Dunbar's lifelike plantation images came from actual scenes of nature, the cabins and roads, the old farms and fences bearing clearly the ravages of time. The vivid images spring from the page and beckon the camera to a dozen different "readings" of each verse of the poem. Third, in mirroring the life of the Black family on the plantation engaged in simple daily tasks or performing acts of love between parent and child, the poem and photograph struck a responsive chord in the minds of readers. The images in poem and photograph reflected through a natural setting the change of the seasons or the uncomplicated course of human emotions. Interpreted by persons who were amateurs in photography but not at all inexperienced in human relationships, the Dunbar poems presented provocative scenes that stimulated the members of the Kiquotan Kamera Klub to search the Hampton community for the most appropriate illustration of the lifelike poetic images.[33]

The paternalism and sentimentalism of those who brought the talents of Dunbar into the cultural limelight cannot be defended. Likewise, the attitudes of those members of the

Kiquotan Kamera Klub in 1899 who, camera in hand, sought to portray scenes of the "good old days" cannot be rationalized. They depicted Blacks in the Hampton community who seemed to be typical "uncles" and "aunties," who revealed the kindliness and satisfaction of pleasant relationships between white masters and their servants. Thus the frontispiece of *Poems of Cabin and Field* depicts an old "plantation uncle" wearing a crushed hat, a kind of "dress shirt" pleated down front, a coat of "Prince Albert" styling, and pants held up by suspenders. The face, with typically negroid features, bears a pleasant expression. The firmly closed lips suggest an inclination to smile. But the total expression, the straight upright stance, the direct gaze at the reader discovers nothing that is menial or servile; rather it reveals dignity, determination, and self-assurance, in spite of age and poverty.

Almost every stanza of the eight poems was illustrated by the camera. The scenes and characters are presented through the voice of a Black speaker who sets the atmosphere and specific tone for the poem. That the illustrations are from real scenes around the Hampton school community suggests the imaginative interpretation of picturesque nature and the realistic rendition of true-to-life cabins, rooms, fences. The sentimentalized scenes revealing the whites who live in "de big house" are described in the third stanza of "The Deserted Plantation." The specific image of "de grubbin'-hoe" that is "a-rustin' in de co'nah" along with "de plow" that is "a-trumblin' down in de field' "—all the forlorn tools and implements—joins the silent banjo to underline the desolation and loneliness in the sentimental tradition of Goldsmith's "Deserted Village." Note the rhetorical questions "Whah's de da'kies, dem dat used to be a-dancin' / Ev'ry night befo' de ol' cabin do'?" and similar queries for "de chillun, dem dat used to be a-prancin' / Er a-rollin' in de san' er on de flo'?" Here, as in the following stanza seeking "ol' Uncle Mordecai or Uncle Aaron" and "Aunt Doshy, Sam an' Kit," are ample opportunities for camera shots of older men and women of the community as well as of children seen playing in the sand. Usually the men were pictured as farmers standing on a bit of furrowed ground, or sitting near a cabin whose unpainted boards suggest the passage of the years. The banjo has found its place among the old, forsaken symbols of happier days gone by. Nature asserts her role in the dreary scene of weeds "growin' green an' rank an' tall" in place of fields where 'de co'n was allus wavin'." All in all the mournful, sentimentalized recollections of the speaker in the poem are fully interpreted by pictures which the camera club spent several months assembling.

The poem most industriously illustrated by club members, according to their records, "Chris'mus is a-Comin'," must have given author and publisher some concern.[34] The usual competitive work on this poem is suggested by the Kiquotan Kamera Klub minutes of January 21, 1899, where it is recorded that for the Dunbar book the club wished to add "Chris'mus is a-Comin'," a poem published in the December issue of the *Bookman.* It appears that this addition was necessary in view of the feeling that several other poems which the publisher seems to have suggested were deemed too difficult to illustrate. Apparently the club members sought poems whose meaning was expressed through sensory images that suggested color, panoramic scene, detail, and line in such a manner that the camera could translate the vision created by the poem into a picture on the page. It is also evident that Dunbar reviewed the pictures which the club offered as illustration of his words, because handwritten notes in the dummy read: "Mr. Dunbar says *no* to the first picture" (referring to one which appears in full page following the title of the poem). The full-page picture of a landscape snow scene must have seemed to Dunbar less specifically a Christmas picture, for the print that he recommended more definitely reflects the Christmas holiday.[35] The scene is inside the "Big House" where the mistress is decorating with holly wreaths and pine branches. The lady is standing on a stool at the window, while an old "uncle" holds more holly for her. On the floor in front of the spacious fireplace a little white boy plays, completing a typical plantation tableau.

The setting and scene of "Chris'mus is a-Comin'," when considered in the context of notes on the dummy, reveal clearly the critical ideals which the photographers sought in their illustrations. Remarks suggest that the first picture—that of an old man standing against a barn—was the best of several candidates for the following lines:

> Bones a gittin' achy,
> Back a-feelin' col',
> Han's a-growin' shaky,
> Jes' lak I was ol'.

Perhaps the "Fros' erpon de meddah" and "Snowdraps lak a feddah" were the integral parts of the background to which the full-page snow scene rejected by Dunbar was directed. In the second stanza the plantation tradition emerges in all its sentimental romanticism:

> Little mas' a-axin',
> "Who is Santy Claus?"
> Meks it kin' o' taxin'
> Not to brek de laws.

Here the illustration is a scene at the corner of what might be identified today as the President's House on the Hampton Institute campus, serving as background for two figures—an old black man and a little white boy who looks up inquiringly at the old uncle.

One of Dunbar's most popular poems appeared as the third poem chosen for illustration in this first illustrated Dunbar edition. The camera club had placed it as sixth in its plan for publication, and had given "Chris'mus is a-Comin' " the second spot. The reader is impressed by the many pictures of children that appear throughout the illustrations because Dunbar seems to have stressed love and affection within the black family. The speaker in "A Banjo Song" frequently refers to his family:

> Den my fam'ly gadders roun' me
> In de fadin' o' de light
>
> .　.　.　.　.
>
> An my wife an' all de othahs,—
> Male an' female, small an' big,—
>
> .　.　.　.　.
>
> Den we all th'ow in our voices
> Fu' to he'p de chune out too,
> Lak a big camp-meetin' choiry
> Tryin' to sing a mou'nah th'oo.

Maintaining this focus on the whole family but paying particular attention to the youngest, "Little Brown Baby" was a favorite oral presentation for many years. The poem possesses those qualities very necessary for the illustrator in that it uses the dramatic device of dialogue, the speaker participating directly in the action. Here the father speaks. Within the poem are specific guidelines for the photographic illustration: "brown baby," "sparkling eyes," sticky syrupy hands, and first teeth showing with dimpled chin in a frequent good-natured smile. But the illustrations for this favorite poem are disappointing. The "brown baby" is an attractive small child, dressed in the style of his day, which did not distinguish the sexes until a child was several years beyond the toddler. However, in the close-up photograph which occupies the full page introducing the poem is a youngster whose expression is pensive, bearing little evidence of the "sparkle" in his eyes, or the bright smile showing the teeth and dimples. For later stanzas the dramatic element is reflected in the pictures illustrating the action when the father suggests that we "tho'w him outen de do' in de san' " and wishes to give him "way to de big buggah-man." In the last stanza the illustration showing the baby clinging to the father's neck precisely pantomimes the thought:

> Dah, now, I t'ought dat you'd hug me close.
>   Go back, ol' buggah, you shan't have dis boy,
> He ain't no tramp, ner no straggler, of co'se;
>   He's pappy's pa'dner an' playmate an' joy.

"Hunting Song" provides out-of-door setting with special emphasis on many of the sensory impressions which the six photographs are unable to capture except as they suggest atmosphere or tone for such lines as

> Tek a cool night, good an' cleah . . .

> Jes' 'bout fall-time o' de yeah
>   W'en de leaves is dry an' brown;
> Tek a dog an' tek a axe,
>   Tek a lantu'n in yo' han',
> Step light whah de switches cracks,
>   Fu' dey's huntin' in de lan'.
> Down th'oo de valleys an' ovah de hills,
>   Into de woods whah de 'simmon-tree grows.

Sounds abound—the horn blown loud and strong so that "de hills an' trees / Sen's de echoes tumblin' back," dogs barking at the scent of "Mistah 'Possum" and "Mistah Coon." All of this takes place in the light of the moon on a clear night when the speaker, an experienced hunter who distinguishes the difference in a dog's bark when he has treed his prey, envisions the brown roasted possum—a favorite of the plantation blacks, according to folk tales. The skill of the poet in appealing to olfactory and tactile senses creates a mood and tone which move beyond the visual camera image.

On rainy days there is "Time to Tinker 'Roun'," mending harness for the mule and really enjoying the opportunity to catch up on chores. Again the dramatic voice of the poem characterizes very clearly the speaker through his soliloquy:

> Den you men's de mule's ol' ha'ness,
> An' you men's de broken chair.
> Hummin' all de time you's wo'kin'
> Some ol' common kind o'air.

Illustrations for this poem appear to have been less difficult. Notes in the dummy suggest that familiar persons in the Hampton community posed for the pictures. The published pictures differ from those submitted to the committee for the dummy. The first picture reveals an older man mending harness in the doorway of a barn; a portion of a wagonwheel is visible at the door amidst trash or scraps of harness realistically littering the floor. The picture published is less striking, portraying a younger man in working clothes near the doorway of a workroom—a scene which easily could have originated in the Harness Shop on the Hampton campus, in view of the penciled note "Captain Moton made substitute." Perhaps the words of the poem, offering many varieties of sensory images, stimulated the imagination of such accomplished amateur photographers as Capt. Robert Russa Moton, thereby eliciting so many illustrations that the camera club committee judged several nominations worthy of inclusion.

In the first meeting of the club for the school year 1899–1900, the club asked its Executive Committee to "continue correspondence with Dodd and Mead, publishers," although the attention of the club was focused on such matters as the very

real probability of building a small clubhouse on the campus of
Hampton Institute. At the club meeting approximately a year
later, on October 26, 1900, "Mr. Rogers reported on plans for
building a clubhouse, and that he and Dr. Frissell were to
locate the exact site this fall, permission for such a building having been given by the Faculty." It is obvious that the Kiquotan
Kamera Klub had a full schedule of activities in the fall of 1900
with discussions about the clubhouse occupying the center
stage, and the individual photographic contributions to such
contests as that sponsored by the *Ladies Home Journal* occasionally coming to the forefront. The committee which had
been appointed to plan the year's photography projects recommended that the club undertake

1. To make illustrations for Dunbar's poem "Fishin'" before
   December 1st
2. To help carry out Dr. Frissell's wish to obtain the teacher's pictures
   by making amateur portraits
3. To make booklets of photographs of Southern Negro types for
   sale[36]

On November 9, when the club met at the "Nutshell" to
consider more carefully its possibilities as a clubhouse, it also
voted to submit pictures for Dunbar's poem "Fishin'" at the
next meeting, November 23. The records show that four negatives for "Fishin'" were submitted, but the club took no action
on these prints. In the meantime, working to arrange a substitute building as a clubhouse and also endeavoring to fulfill
commitments for negatives, the club found itself frustrated and
its plans thwarted when the faculty changed its mind in regard
to allowing the club to use the "Nutshell." However, one bright
gleam filtered through the clouds of confusion and dissatisfac-
tion by way of "a proposition from Dodd, Mead and Co., who
wished to know if the Camera Club would undertake to
illustrate a book of Dunbar's poems similar to his 'Cabin and
Field' and containing about the same number of pictures."
With this offer under discussion, the club appears to have
found the stimulation it needed. Therefore, "at a special meeting on February 11, 1901, the club voted unanimously to undertake the illustration of the new book for Dodd, Mead & Co.

on condition that [the club] receive $200.00 for the entire work
and that [they] have until July 1st to finish it."

In planning to illustrate the new Dunbar book, the Kiquotan
Kamera Klub was better organized than previously. They had
learned from the experience of working with the publication of
Poems of Cabin and Field. On March 13, at a special meeting to
discuss financial arrangements with Dodd, Mead and Company, "Miss Davis brought in a set of illustrations for 'At
Candle-Lightin' Time,' and Miss Herron, Mr. Miner, and Mr.
Brown were appointed a committee to act upon them." In addition to this arrangement, "it was thought best that each member
of the club have a copy of all the poems, and that someone be
employed to make these copies."

At the regular club meeting in March the group made
specific assignments of committees to provide illustrations of
each of the poems which the club had selected, thereby fixing
responsibility for the work. In general three persons were
assigned to a poem and deadlines were established. Apparently
this plan was productive because most readers agreed that the
second illustrated collection of poems was superior to the
earlier collection. Concurring with this opinion, the *Southern
Workman* in its section on "Hampton Incidents" concluded "that
the photographic work in this instance is an improvement over
that in the previous book" and quoted the *Dial* as commenting
favorably upon the new illustrated book:

Mr. Paul Laurence Dunbar has already won wide recognition as a
poet, using the dialect of his race. A selection of nine of these poems,
bearing the name, "Candle-Lightin' Time" which is beautifully
illustrated with photography by the Hampton Institute Camera Club,
and with marginal decorations by Miss Margaret Armstrong will be
likely to win him fresh popularity. The book also reveals the great
possibilities of artistic photography for purposes of illustration. No
studied "composition by the engraver or etcher could surpass some of
these glimpses of picturesque nature, or the poses of the human
figures.[37]

Books of this type frequently become cherished gifts, and
Candle-Lightin' Time came off the press at a most appropriate
time for Christmas shopping, according to the reviewers.[38] The

Illustration for Paul Laurence Dunbar's "When dey 'Listed Colored Soldiers"
in *Candle-Lightin' Time*

poems were bound in a handsome little book and the illustrations of the opening poem, "Dinah Kneading Dough," struck
many readers as pleasantly as they affected the reviewer of the
book in the *Dial,* who said that "the three interiors and one
landscape . . . are enough to establish the artistic value of the
book, and those following are equally good." The frontispiece
is the photograph of a Black woman dressed in the customary
long gathered skirt and white shirtwaist of the period, carrying
in her right hand a candle in a holder, shielding the candle with
her left hand. Her head is covered with a scarf, her black face is
attractive, showing rather regular features, and her eyes look
directly at the reader. Appearing again in a different pose at
the end of the book, this figure underlines the theme of family
unity and love "At Candle-Lightin' Time." According to the
plan of the camera club, from four to six pictures were selected
to illustrate each poem. Usually key words or lines of especially
strong visual imagery gave the photographer his clue, since the
poems are all relatively short.

Candle-Lightin' Time offered nine poems that had appeared in a variety of periodicals, such as the *Saturday Evening Post,* which published "Lullaby," and the *Southern Workman,* which illustrated the poem "Fishin' " in the January 1901 issue. The first poem in this collection is different from those in *Poems of Cabin and Field* as well as the remaining poems in *Candle-Lightin' Time,* both in content, style, and illustration. This poem focuses on a beautiful Black girl, pert, lively, bright-eyed, seen at first in full-page portrait standing in front of an open fireplace, one hand placed saucily on her hip, the other on the mantel as though she is on the verge of a flippant remark. This must be Dinah, whose young admirer praises her beauty, which seems enhanced by such domestic chores as kneading dough. More significant in the discussion of this poem is the fact that it is written in Standard English—the only poem in the illustrated editions not written in dialect. Yet it focuses on the favorite Dunbar themes, love and nature, with the latter yielding to love:

> I have seen full many a sight
> Born of day or drawn by night:
> Sunlight on a silver stream,
> Golden lillies all a-dream,
> Lofty mountains, bold and proud
> Veiled beneath the lacelike cloud;
> But no lovely sight I know
> Equals Dinah kneading dough.

Rejecting the beauties of nature, the lover is enchanted by the sight of Dinah engaged in everyday tasks. The tetrameter couplets continue to detail the physical attractions of the "dainty maid" who possessed "eyes of jet and teeth of pearl."[39] The photographs clearly portray the charming Dinah as she works, "Brown arms buried elbow-deep / Their domestic rhythm keep," thus embellishing the duties of simple, real life with the allurements of her personality.

The other love poem in this illustrated collection, "A Spring Wooing," fulfills the promise of the title by intermingling a poet's keen sensitivity to the myriad signs of awakening nature with the incipient feelings of love:

Illustration for Paul Laurence Dunbar's "Dinah Kneading Dough" in *Candle-Lightin' Time*

> Come on walkin' wid me, Lucy; 'tain't no time to mope erroun'
>   W'en de sunshine's shoutin' glory in de sky,
> An' de little Johnny-Jump-Ups jes' a-springin' f'om de groun',
>   Den a-lookin' roun' to ax each othah w'y.

Obviously, members of the Kiquotan Kamera Klub located ample scenes for pictures of spring in Hampton, Virginia. There the luxuriant foliage half hiding the cabins and farmhouses, brought vivid color—the pink and white dogwood, the yellow forsythia, the red, pink, white, and purple azaleas served as picturesque background for the strolling couples.

In contrast to these poems in which the lovers speak their feeling respectively for the young ladies Dinah and Lucy, the other poem in this collection dealing with young love is pragmatic and humorous. The voice of the poem is that of the prospective "father of the bride," who finally recalls his own youth when he "cou'ted Sally Jane," and ceases grumbling about propping up "The Old Front Gate":

> W'en de hinges creak an' cry,
>   An' de bahs go slantin' down,
> You kin reckon dat hit's time
>   Fu' to cas' yo' eye erroun',
> 'Cause daih ain' no 'sputin' dis,
>   Hit's de trues' sign to show,
> Dat daih's cou'tin' goin' on
>   W'en de ol' front gate sags low.

The photograph illustrating the last verse brings together the daughter, her young man, and her parents on the steps at the door of a very primitive cabin, perhaps to relieve the old front gate that will "keep on saggin' low" until all "de gals is ma'ied off."

The very favorable review of *Candle-Lightin' Time* in the December issue of the *Southern Workman* suggested the interest aroused in these poems of simple homelife among Black people and pointed out the similarities to *Poems of Cabin and Field:* "All the contents are new [that is, never previously anthologized]. 'A Spring Wooing' and 'Song of Summer' take the place of the Christmas and Thanksgiving lyrics; there is 'Fishin' ' instead of 'Huntin' ' and 'The Little Brown Baby' has a 'Lullaby' all to herself. . . . The tragedies brought by war to both races on the old plantation touch our hearts anew in 'When dey 'Listed Colored Soldiers'."[40] Dramatic contrasts of Blacks with whites, between soldiers in blue and soldiers in gray, highlight the emotions of the Black girl whose low-key account suggests the pain and suffering of the war-ravaged plantation people, the Blacks as well as the whites:

> Bofe my mastahs went in gray suits, an' I loved de Yankee blue,
> But I t'ought dat I could sorrer for de losin' of 'em too;
> But I couldn't, for I did n't know de ha'f o' whut I saw,
> Twell dey 'listed colo'ed sojers an' my 'Lias went to wah.

In two other poems Dunbar creates vivid scenes from homely, everyday affairs on the plantation. These scenes evoked from members of the camera club an unusual number of choices for illustration. Although only seven illustrations tell the story of "Dat Ol' Mare O' Mine," the members of the club had found the poem very suggestive for photography. It is said that Dunbar used a mare during his stay in Colorado and that he developed the poem from that experience. Humor, realism, and perception of the understanding between a man and a particular animal abound as the narrator describes Sukey's responses:

> Ef you pull her on de lef' han' she plum 'termined to go right,
> A cannon could n't skeer huh, but she boun' to tek a fright
> At a piece o' common paper, or anyt'ing dat's white,
>   Dat ol' mare o' mine.

"At Candle-Lightin' Time" the title poem of the collection, stresses a theme Dunbar repeated many times in his interpretation of the plantation tradition. This theme emerges in his conception of the unifying elements in the Black family—the love of the father for his children, the time he spends with them after his workday, his storytelling which involves animal tales and folklore.

Featured in this poem is the scene at the close of the day, when the father uses his hands to "mek de shadders on de wall." Describing Mistah Rabbit whose ears loom large in the "shadders," the father entertains his brood, using a type of folk imagination, to the extent of conjuring "de buga-man!" The familiar symbol of the banjo brings a happy ending to the "play acting," evicting the "buga-man" and sending the children off to sleep.

On January 5, 1902, the Kiquotan Kamera Klub held a special meeting, with seventeen members present, during which "the work committee reported the offer of Dodd, Mead & Co. to have the club illustrate a new book of Mr. Dunbar's poems." Discussion of the proposal brought suggestions that "the competition be divided between the members doing the work and the club." Following the usual procedure of reading and discussing the poems in the meetings, each member was asked to hand to the secretary a list of those poems he considered suitable for illustration. Throughout January 1902 the club was busy negotiating with Dodd, Mead and Company. They agreed on the publisher's offer and requested that the club be allowed to set up a plan for arrangement of the poems in the book. When "Mr. Miner suggested that the club ask for permission to make a dummy of the book as we prepare to illustrate it," members began to establish more specific regulations for illustrating the new collection. Learning from experience with the two previously illustrated volumes, the club no doubt realized the problems that could arise in the preparation of a larger group of illustrations. A committee was appointed to have charge of the general arrangement of the book and to submit to the club a plan for each poem. It was voted that final decision on pictures be made by the whole club at the regular weekly meetings after pictures had been submitted, numbered, and placed on exhibition for more than one evening. Selection of pictures was made by ballot. Each member of the club would submit an itemized bill when the period for making pictures had passed. By February, 1903, it appears that Miner had conferred directly with the publishers, explaining plans of the camera club on such details as the title and the possible introduction of color.

It was not until October 12, 1903, that the club completed its illustrations for the Dunbar book that would be called *When Malindy Sings*. At that time eighty pictures had been accepted by the publishers. According to the club minutes, "Mrs. Brown reported her interview with Mr. Dodd concerning the book, during which its merits were generally discussed and all the pictures criticized favorably. In comparison with previous books, Mr. Dodd expressed his opinion that this last is the best." Apparently the dummy was in the possession of the publishers because Mrs. Brown reported that she had "asked for the sample book we loaned them. Mr. Dodd asked if he could keep it until their book was definitely planned. The request was granted."[41]

The number of poems requiring illustration in *When Malindy Sings* was greater than twice the combined number of the two volumes previously illustrated. In this collection are some of the best-loved Dunbar poems, including the title poem of the volume. The review in the *Southern Workman,* December 1903, was indeed favorable:

As an illustration of Mr. Dunbar's insight into human nature and especially that found under the brown skin of his people, this latest volume of verses is eminently satisfactory. They are rollicking, pathetic, amusing, sad, sentimental, clever, weird, and altogether charming. The volume is uniform with *Candle-Lightin' Time* and *Poems of Cabin and Field,* being illustrated, as they were, by the Hampton Institute Camera Club. The decorations in this volume are by Margaret Armstrong and consist of slightly conventionalized flowers and vines outlined in light blue. . . . The illustrations are perhaps even better than those in the two previous books, being less literal and showing more artistic power as well as better workmanship. . . . Some of the illustrations are deserving of special mention. . . . Those in "Two Little Boots" show the greatest power and feeling.[42]

As implied in this review, the poems in *When Malindy Sings* explore various moods and scenes that reflect the human personality as Dunbar perceived it. Colored by vivid images that create joy and sadness, humor or satire, realism or romance, each of the twenty poems provides insights into, and perspectives on, the familiar and the strange, intermingled in a fresh and unique combination. If the poems are grouped according to the subjects which Dunbar frequently portrayed, and if it is recognized that the dialect written by Dunbar is equally adept at portraying character and scene simultaneously through dialogue or individual musings, the reader may easily perceive the basis for considering this volume the best of the illustrated collections.

   Dunbar presents his love of nature in at least five poems relating to different aspects of nature. With two exquisite photographs suggesting spring in Virginia, the forsythia and dogwood again coming alive through descriptions of wooded landscapes, the poem "Spring Fever" portrays a speaker who suffers from the common disease of the season:

> Grass commence a-comin'
>   Thoo de thawin' groun',
> Evah bird dat whistles
>   Keepin' noise erroun';
>
>   . . . . .
>
> Bluebird sass de robin,
>   Robin sass him back,
> Den de bluebird scol' him
>   'Twell his face is black.

And yet a "Warm Day in Winter" suggests

> "Sunshine in de medders,
>   Greenness on de way;
> Dat's de blessed reason
>   I sing all de day."

But the poet who wrote "Drizzle" had not only a keen appreciation for nature in sun and rain but also a penetrating sensitivity to human nature in its many aspects and nuances:

> Hit's been drizzlin' an' been sprinklin',
>   Kin' o' techy all day long.
> I ain't wet enough fu' toddy,
>   I's too damp to raise a song,
> An' de case have set me t'inkin',
>   Dat dey's folk des lak de rain,
> Dat does drizzlin' w'en dey's talkin',
>   An' won't speak out flat an' plain.
>
> Ain't you nevah set an' listened
>   At a body 'splain his min'?
> W'en de t'oughts dey keep on drappin'
>   Was n't big enough to fin'?

These "drizzlin' people," philosophizes the speaker, "mek no mo' 'pression / Den dis powd'ry kin' o' rain" and offer no substance to a conversation. They fail to "speak out nachul," and this commentator on life has learned to prefer those outspoken folks "Whut'll say des whut dey mean."

As anticipated in a volume of Dunbar verses, there are several poems whose major theme is love and courtship in the Black community. These poems portray a different level of rural beauty in the middle-class setting, not now a broken-down "front gate" or crude cabin. The lines of "The Lookin' Glass" demand that the camera focus on a beautiful young lady, one fit to rival Miss Alice Moore, whose charms captured the heart of young Paul Dunbar. In the poem the flirtatious beauty entertains guests and smiles enchantingly into the mirror which the lover envies: "while she sasshey 'roun' an' bow, / Smilin' den an' poutin' now." In contrast to this sophisticated beauty who tantalizes the young man, Mandy Lou, the heroine of "A Plantation Portrait," is equally attractive in a wooded setting. Her personal charms are delicate and modest, suggesting serenity of spirit complementing the beauty of face and form:

> Eyes ez big an' roun' an' bright
>   Ez de light
> Whut de moon gives in de prime
>   Harvest time.

Of the poems that attracted most attention and seemed to bring greatest pleasure to the greatest number of Dunbar readers and listeners, three became immediate favorites. One of these lyrics depicts the grief upon the death of a child. Concerning human grief and sadness, Paul Laurence Dunbar had full knowledge from his personal experiences. As a poet he could depict a mother's grief in the touching words of "Two Little Boots," which symbolizes the poignancy of the loss endured by mothers who have been separated from, or who have lost, their children:

> Somehow, you don' seem so gay,
>   Po' little boots,
> Sence yo' ownah went erway,
>   Po' little boots!

Yo' bright tops don' look so red,
Dese brass tips is dull an' dead;
"Goo'-by," whut de baby said;
Deah little boots!

Dunbar frequently expressed a special regard for children in his personal life as well as in his poetry. From "Little Brown Baby" to "The Boogah Man" and "Wadin' in de Creek," he immortalized the love of parents for their offspring, and in "Two Little Boots" he depicts sympathetically the sad recollections of a grief-stricken mother.

On the other hand, the main, continuing spirit of Dunbar's poems about children in the verses of these illustrated editions is love within the Black family, with gaiety and laughter, humor and fun as dominant characteristics. Expressing these qualities in his most creative way, the poet dramatizes vividly a family scene in one of his most famous humorous poems, "In the Morning." The interaction between mother and son, and the comic elements of the situation have made this dramatic monologue a favorite for oral presentations. The single slice of life with its tight, climactic organization brings the short scene to a conclusion as 'Lias finds that his hands are not quicker than his mother's eyes.

In all of the Dunbar poems music becomes an integral part, either in the use of melody and rhythm as major components of his verse or in the use of musical instruments as subject of the verse. Dunbar's keen sense of rhythm and his ear for music make his poems adaptable to musical scores and also transform the verses into rhythmical explications of Black folklife. In almost every collection Dunbar includes a tribute to, or comment on, a musical instrument—the banjo, the fiddle or the violin, an instrument the poet himself played. In this third illustrated volume he personifies the instrument as a beautiful woman, "My Sweet Brown Gal," and thus reveals his deep affection for the rhythm and "Old Tunes."

In another poem "The Colored Band" marches "down de street," stepping smartly to the rhythm, "Fu' de music dat dey mekin' can't be beat." However, the most famous and probably the best-liked Dunbar poem reflecting musical interest is the popular "When Malindy Sings," the title poem of this volume. The poem is illustrated by four pictures, one of which shows a young white girl sitting at the piano looking up at a well-dressed Black man standing near by and talking to her, seeming to say

> G'way an' quit dat noise, Miss Lucy—
>   Put dat music book away;
> What's de use to keep on tryin'?
>   Ef you practise twell you're gray,
> You cain't sta't no notes a-flyin'
>   Lak de ones dat rants and rings
> F'om de kitchen to de big woods
>   When Malindy sings
>
>   .   .   .   .   .
>
> But fu' real melojous music,
>   Dat jes' strikes yo' hea't and clings,
> Jes' you stan' an' listen wif me
>   When Malindy sings.

For oral reading this poem rivaled "In the Morning" as a piece in which the dramatic reader could vocalize the hymns "Come to Jesus" and "Rock of Ages," cited in the sixth stanza, thereby giving the oral reading even more realism than what emerges from the page. Some biographers have concluded that Dunbar paid tribute to his adored mother, Matilda Dunbar, in this vivid portrayal of Malindy singing.

The three illustrated collections—*Poems of Cabin and Field, Candle-Lightin' Time,* and *When Malindy Sings*—were well received by the reading public, according to the reviews and notices in popular periodicals and newspapers. In referring to *Candle-Lightin' Time,* the New York *Observer,* December 5, 1901, commented that "Dunbar is a real poet and his homely rhymes are as true to Nature's heart as those of Robert Burns, whom he resembles." Continuing his assessment of *Candle-Lightin' Time,* the reviewer asserted that "this book is a striking proof of what the black man can do in poetry and art, Margaret Armstrong's decorations being the only white work in the volume." Obviously, the reviewer was unaware that the Hampton Institute staff and the Kiquotan Kamera Klub included black and white members.

The next three illustrated volumes continued the conventional style of illustrated poems popularized by *Poems of Cabin and Field.* These later volumes appeared in successive years: *Li'l Gal,* in 1904, offering twenty-two poems; *Howdy, Honey, Howdy!,* 1905, presenting twenty-one poems; *Joggin' Erlong,* 1906, featuring twenty poems. Dodd, Mead and Company continued as publisher, but the illustrations were provided by one member of the Kiquotan Kamera Klub, Leigh Richmond Miner. Decorations for all but the last volume remained in the hands of Margaret Armstrong. John Rae created the decorations for *Joggin' Erlong.*

This last illustrated edition was published in October following the death of Dunbar in February 1906 and from all evidence was prepared for publication with the poet's cooperation and advice. Miner, its illustrator, had worked with the earlier photographic illustrations arranged by the club and was actively involved in the work on *When Malindy Sings.* The camera club minutes record that at the regular meeting on October 21, 1907, the nominating committee presented a slate of officers headed by the name of Leigh Richmond Miner for president. After a unanimous vote, however, Miner found it necessary to offer his resignation, which was accepted with regret.

Leigh Richmond Miner, who came to Hampton Institute in 1898 as an art teacher, was, like Dunbar, "a builder of beauty," according to the *Norfolk Journal and Guide* in its tribute upon his death in June 1935. Similar to the famous poet whose writings he so well illustrated, Miner is described as "a quiet efficient worker, who not only wrote poetry but transmitted it into lovely arrangements of walks, bowers, and stately trees." Because of his tastes, temperament, and professional competence as both a poet and visual artist, Miner best understood the sensitive insights and clearly etched images that Dunbar projected. Admirably suited for this demanding task, Miner used the camera creatively to translate into pictures Dunbar's poetic world of work and play and to convey the feelings of love, joy, and sorrow experienced by Black people in the South. Keenly aware of form, color, and design in the settings of nature and in the compositions by man, Leigh Miner was able to undertake an assignment that had originally taxed the productivity of approximately twenty to twenty-five club members. Miner would carry to completion the activity that had brought to the club and the school significant national notice and had served as a source of inspiration, interest, and entertainment to Black and white readers alike. These last illustrated volumes were being circulated while Dunbar was in failing health, and at a time when his suffering had elicited the concern and sympathy of hundreds of his readers.[43]

Dunbar as well as his admirers realized that his poetic genius would soon cease. Each poem dictated, "Joggin' Erlong," for example, was in a sense distilled from his life's blood, and therefore more precious.[44] Artist-photographer Leigh Miner must have spent many thoughtful hours in illustrating these last Dunbar poems. Miner symbolizes the long reach of the Dunbar poetic genius—a reach that extended far beyond the seaside campus of Hampton and the Virginia community, across racial and geographic boundaries into the hearts and minds of responsive human beings wherever they found his words. Dunbar spoke not only to the artistic temperament such as that possessed by Leigh Miner but also to semiliterate Black people who, particularly at this time in their racial history, yearned for one who could voice their joys and sorrows, their hopes and longings. The first Black professional poet—"a poet of his people"—Dunbar said to them:

> Be proud, my Race, in mind and soul;
> Thy name is writ on Glory's scroll
>   In characters of fire.
> High 'mid the clouds of Fame's bright sky
> Thy banner's blazoned folds now fly,
> And truth shall lift them higher.

Notes

1. Benjamin Griffith Brawley, "Dunbar Memorial Service," *Voice of the Negro* 3, no. 4 (1906), 244.

2. *Southern Workman* 35 (1906), 137.

3. Lida Keck Wiggins, "Den of a Literary Lion," *Voice of the Negro* 3, no. 1 (1906), 50.

4. *Journal of Negro History* 23 (1932), 400.

5. Dumas Malone and Basil Rauch, *The New Nation: 1865–1917* (New York: Appleton-Century-Crofts, 1960), pp. 195–98.

6. John A. Garraty, *Interpreting American History: Conversations with Historians* (New York: Macmillan, 1970), pt. 2, p. 52.

7. Kenneth Stampp, "Triumph of White Racism," in *Blacks in White America since 1865: Issues and Interpretations,* ed. Robert C. Twombly (New York: David McKay Co., 1971), p. 52.

8. Lester H. Fishel, Jr., and Benjamin Quarles, eds., *The Negro American: A Documentary History* (Glenview, Ill.: Scott, Foresman, 1967), p. 332.

9. Darwin Turner, "Paul Laurence Dunbar: The Poet and the Myths," *CLA Journal* 19 (1974), p. 157.

10. Addison Gayle, *Oak and Ivy* (New York: Doubleday and Co., 1971), pp. 72–75.

11. *The Complete Poems of Paul Laurence Dunbar* (New York: Dodd, Mead and Co., 1913), p. 14.

12. Benjamin Brawley, *Paul Laurence Dunbar: Poet of His People* (Chapel Hill: Univ. North Carolina Press, 1936), pp. 40–41 (italics mine).

13. Virginia Cunningham, *Paul Laurence Dunbar and His Song* (New York: Dodd Mead and Co., 1947), p. 186.

14. Hollis B. Frissell Papers, Archives, Hampton Institute, Hampton, Va.

15. Ibid.

16. Ibid.

17. Frissell to *Southern Workman* contributors, Jan. 18, 1899.

18. Garraty, *Interpreting American History,* pt. 2, p. 51.

19. Minutes of the Kiquotan Kamera Klub, Oct. 21, 1893, Kiquotan Kamera Klub Papers, Archives, Hampton Institute (hereafter cited as Minutes; references are by date and, when appropriate, by page). The name is variously spelled, but this seems to be the preferred spelling.

20. Ibid.

21. Cunningham, *Dunbar,* p. 99.

22. *Voice of the Negro* 3, no. 4 (1906), 271.

23. Minutes, Oct. 27, 1893.

24. Hellmut Lehman-Haupt, *The Book in America: A History of Book Making, Selling and the Collecting of Books in the United States* (New York: R. R. Bowker Co., 1939), pp. 78, 287.

25. Ibid., p. 287.

26. Cunningham, *Dunbar,* p. 153.

27. Gilman J. Martin Geindo, March 27, 1973, Eleanor Gilman Papers, Archives, Hampton Institute.

28. At the exhibit on April 15, 1898, one of the framed works "contained the joint work of the club in a collection of scenes illustrating the 'Introduction' of Whittier's 'Tent on the Beach.' " (*Home Bulletin* [newspaper published by the Veterans Administration and printed by Hampton Institute Press], April 15, 1898, clipping attached to the Minutes).

29. Minutes, Jan. 21, 1899, pp. 43–44.

30. *Southern Workman* 28 (1899), 229.

31. Minutes, 1899, p. 46.

32. The dummy of *Cabin and Field* in the Archives of Hampton Institute, with its handwritten initials and notes, implies the variety of opinion, the questions raised, and the veto power of the author in such a comment as "Mr. Dunbar says 'no' to the second one." The club seems to have planned that the book begin with "Hunting Song" and end with "The Deserted Plantation" along with other changes in the order of the poems; "Little Brown Baby" is number six in this arrangement; last is "Chris'mus is a-Comin'."

33. Turner, "Dunbar: The Poet," pp. 155–71.

34. Minutes, Jan. 21, 1899, pp. 43–44.

35. Dummy of *Poems of Cabin and Field*, Kiquotan Kamera Klub Papers.

36. Minutes, March 13, 1901.

37. "Hampton Incidents," *Southern Workman* 31 (1902), 40, quotes the *Dial*.

38. Cunningham, *Dunbar*, p. 227.

39. Turner, "Dunbar: The Poet," p. 156 and passim.

40. Helen A. Ludlow, review of *Candle-Lightin' Time*, *Southern Workman* 30 (1901), 697.

41. There is no dummy in Archives, Hampton Institute, for *When Malindy Sings*.

42. *Southern Workman* 32 (1903), 630.

43. New York *Herald*, Oct. 16, 1904. "Paul Dunbar Began Rhyming at Six—Negro Poet, Who is Dying, Showed Early Signs of His Genius—Proud of African Blood," in "Paul Laurence Dunbar," Peabody Room Clipping File, no. 48, Hampton Institute, Hampton, Va.

44. New York *Sun*, Oct. 16, 1904. "To Finish His Drama Dunbar's Only Ambition," ibid.

William H. Sheppard:
Fighter for African Rights
Larryetta M. Schall

IN 1910 UPON his return from the Congo, where he had spent the previous twenty years, Dr. William H. Sheppard was at least as well known as his schoolmate Booker T. Washington.[1] Washington remains famous; Sheppard has fallen into oblivion, his personal courage and his active participation in the struggle for African rights remembered by only a few historians and theologians. Washington was concerned primarily with the plight of the Black man in America, particularly in the South; Sheppard, with his plight in Africa. Washington was concerned primarily with his secular education, "education for life"; Sheppard with his religious education, "education for life" and after. Both men, however, brought many of the same ideas and attitudes to their work. Both attended Hampton Institute in the late nineteenth century and acquired the same educational philosophy. Each was deeply influenced by Hampton, a theme that Sheppard constantly returns to in his letters, addresses, and other writings.

Sheppard was the first Black missionary to be sent to the Congo, where he served from 1890 to 1910.[2] As a young man just out of Stillman Institute, the Southern Presbyterian Theological Seminary for Colored Men at Tuscaloosa, Alabama, with a pastorate in Atlanta, William H. Sheppard applied to the Southern Presbyterian Church to be sent as a missionary to Africa, although no Black missionaries had previously been assigned there. In 1890 Sheppard's request was granted, and he was assigned to go to the Congo Free State, West Central Africa, with Samuel N. Lapsley, the son of Judge Lapsley of Alabama, a young white minister also just out of seminary.[3]

Both left for the Congo from New York in March 1890, sailing on the *Adriatic* to Liverpool, then proceeding by train to London. There they outfitted themselves with all the supplies they thought necessary to their survival in Africa: "cowrie

William H. Sheppard with African warriors

shells, beads, salt and brass wire [all to be used as
money] . . . flour, sugar, butter and lard; also thin linen clothing and helmets for the sun."⁴ Taking a train to Harwich, then
a steamer to Rotterdam, they boarded the *Afrikaan,* a small
Dutch trading ship, which docked at Shark's Point at the mouth
of the Congo after a three-week voyage. Lapsley and Sheppard
continued up the great river, stopping at Boma, then capital of
the Congo Free State, until they came to Matadi, where they
had to leave the river to trek overland to Stanley Pool, a walk of
250 miles through dense underbrush and across rivers. They
left Matadi for Stanley Pool on June 27, 1890, and took a ferry
across the Mpozo River; then, against the earnest advice of the
native bearers, they both decided to swim across the N'Kissy
River, a river infested with crocodiles. When they arrived at
Stanley Pool, the Bateke, a tribe of Bantu, asked Sheppard to
hunt hippopotamuses for meat. On his first hunt Sheppard
shot two. Going out on another hunt, Sheppard shot a third
that was standing in the river. He jumped in, tied a rope
around it to drag it to shore, and, once again, saw crocodile-

infested waters. Altogether, Sheppard and Lapsley killed thirty-six hippopotamuses.

From Stanley Pool they traveled south by steamboat for thirty days until they came to Luebo in the Kassai District of the Congo, where they decided to locate their mission station — 200 miles from Stanley Pool and "1200 miles into the heart of Africa alone," 800 miles from the nearest doctor. They would be isolated among the Bateke until the steamer *Florida* returned in nine months.[5] At Luebo, Sheppard began his singular work. Along with Lapsley, he founded the first day school and Sunday school in the district. There they taught English and Christian principles, while they began to learn the Kassai language in order to translate the Bible.

While beginning their mission, they saw members of the Bakuba tribe trading goods at Luebo and became interested in them because of their "apparent superiority in physique, manners, dress and dialect."[6] The young missionaries found out that the Bakuba, ruled by King Lukenga, a traditional name each king assumed, had a closed society; no strangers were permitted to enter its territory. They decided to study the Bakuba language, learning it from the traders they encountered, preparatory to penetrating the "forbidden land" of the Bakuba. Before the attempt could be made, Lapsley had to leave on government business. While away he contracted fever and died at Matadi in 1892, leaving Sheppard alone at Luebo, the only Westerner within many hundreds of miles. However, Sheppard managed to carry out their plan and journeyed to Ibanj, the capital of the Bakuba, where King Lukenga permitted him to found a second missionary station. Sheppard succeeded in establishing contact with the Bakuba through a fortunate coincidence. The Bakuba believed in reincarnation and took Sheppard, who was Black and could speak their language, as the reincarnated spirit of Bobe Mekabe, one of King Lukenga's sons who had died.[7]

By the time in 1893 when the missionary board of the Southern Presbyterian Church recalled Sheppard to give an account of his mission, he had established missions at Luebo and Ibanj, deeper in the Congo than any other Westerner, even Livingstone, had traveled.[8] He had contacted and made friends of the elusive Bakuba, whom the Belgian government had been trying to contact with no success. On his way home Sheppard stopped in London to lecture to the Royal Geographical Society about the Bakuba and their culture. Because of his discoveries, the society made him a fellow, the first Black American elected F.R.G.S.[9]

In 1894, shortly after he had been recalled by the missionary board, Sheppard was on his way back to Africa with his new wife, the former Lucy Gantt. They settled among the Bakuba at the mission at Ibanj. Soon after their arrival, the Bakuba came to Sheppard for help. A cannibalistic tribe, the Zappo-Zap, was murdering and eating the villagers in Pianga country, and the Bakuba tribesmen called upon Sheppard to stop this slaughter. At first Sheppard felt that he could do nothing, but then he received the following directive from Luebo, mission head-quarters: "Dear Brother Sheppard," it read, "We hear of at-rocities being committed in the Pianga country by the Zappo-Zaps. We commission you immediately on receipt of this letter to go over and stop the raid."[10]

Sheppard managed to get eleven Kassai warriors to accom-pany him on the seemingly impossible mission of stopping seven hundred cannibalistic Zappo-Zaps from terrorizing people in the Bakuba district, fifty thousand of whom, it was estimated, "were hiding in the bush."[11] In a letter Sheppard provides vivid details of his journey to find the cannibals. He tells of a burned village they passed through and of the dead people, nothing left but their skeletons.[12] As Sheppard and his men got closer to the Zappo-Zaps, they saw more burned villages and more "frames." Once again Sheppard was aided by a fortuitous occurrence. As he and his eleven men were being beset by the cannibals, he was recognized by Chembamba, whose life Sheppard had saved two years earlier. Chembamba stopped the attack and guided Sheppard to their stockade, which the natives called the "fatal trap" because no one ever emerged alive. There Sheppard met with Chief Malumba N'kusa, whom he described as "a man who, with his eyebrows shaved off, and his eyelashes pulled out, can yet look at the sun at mid-day without winking; his teeth are filed off to a sharp point; he wears little clothing, is very tall and has a very long neck. He is a most repulsive looking man."[13]

Inside the stockade Sheppard saw a flag flying, and although he does not say it was the Belgian flag, the details he provides strongly suggest that it was. Sheppard asked Malumba N'kusa why he and his people were terrorizing the Bakuba, and the chief admitted that the state sent him to prey on the villagers and destroy those who refused to pay taxes or who did not collect enough rubber.[14] Sheppard also noticed a number of women prisoners whom the Zappo-Zaps were holding as food reserves but was unable to secure their release. Upon his return to Luebo, Sheppard sent a report to the Belgian state post concerning the atrocities that he had witnessed—including row upon row of right hands drying in the sun, which the Zappo-Zaps turned in as proof of the natives they killed—and noted that many women were being kept as prisoners. Upon receipt of this report, the Belgian government did dispatch soldiers who arrested Malumba N'kusa and freed the women. Evidence, however, still points in the direction of Belgian complicity in the inhumane acts performed. Sheppard says that "Malumba N'kusa they put in chains; and as the chains went around him, and they put a strong lock on him, he said, 'You have sent me to do this and yet you have put me in chains!' "[15]

Sheppard exposed these atrocities in his report to the Belgian state post, causing an international furor as the facts became publicized. Article upon article was published in the missionary papers and journals, all protesting this inhumanity and many suggesting that the Congo Free State should be put under the control of the Belgian parliament rather than continue as a private colony of King Leopold II.[16] Among the people moved to respond was Booker T. Washington. In 1904 he detailed these grim horrors in "Cruelty in the Congo," an article based largely on Sheppard's report to the Belgian government.[17]

Interest in Africa, and the Congo in particular, was high because of all of the publicity generated initially by Sheppard and continued by other missionaries. Consequently, during their 1904–5 visit to the United States, the Sheppards were in great

demand for talks about Africa at both Black churches and
white ones. Sheppard was so sought after that President Theodore Roosevelt invited him to visit the White House, where he
"presented to President Roosevelt, a handsome rug, coverlet of
palm fibre linen, and a unique pipe, all of the articles being
manufactured and used by the natives of Central Africa. Sheppard told the President that since he went to Africa the natives
have introduced printing presses and now print the Bible in
their native languages."[18] Sheppard in turn received two
autograph cards while at the White House, each signed by
President Roosevelt. He also was awarded an honorary Doctor
of Divinity degree on June 14, 1905, by Biddle University,
Charlotte, North Carolina, so that he became a D.D. as well as a
F.R.G.S.[19]

Through his 1899 report Sheppard was instrumental in stopping the vicious exploitation of native labor by the Congo Free
State, which used one tribe to control others. This courageous
stand made him famous. Many news commentators regarded
him as a Black hero of the Congo. Nine years later he took
another equally courageous stand against the exploitation of
native laborers by the rubber companies. In January 1908
Sheppard published an article in the *Kassai Herald*, the
magazine of the Southern Presbyterian missionaries in Luebo,
on the condition of the natives, particularly the Bakuba. This
article outraged the Kassai Rubber Company, which lodged
charges against him. Sheppard wrote, in part:

But within these last three years how changed they [the Bakuba
tribesmen] are! Their farms are growing up in weeds and jungle.
Their King is practically a slave, their houses now are mostly only
half-built single rooms, and are much neglected. . . .

Why this change? You have it in a few words. There are armed
sentries of chartered trading companies, who force the men and
women to spend most of their days and nights in the forests making
rubber, and the price they receive is so meagre that they cannot live
upon it.[20]

The Kassai Company, the only chartered trading company in
the district, thought that Sheppard's comment about armed
sentries of trading companies applied directly to it, so it
brought suit against him on September 20, 1909, in the Court

of the First Instance, Leopoldville, "for the recovery of sixteen thousand dollars damages for defamation and injury."[21] The Reverend William M. Morrison, Sheppard's fellow missionary who had been in the Congo since 1896, was also mentioned in the suit, but he was not brought to trial because the clerk miswrote the summons.[22]

The Kassai Company had directed the clerk of the court at Leopoldsville to serve two distinct summons—one on Dr. Morrison for the charges which he had brought against the Company in his correspondence with the former director in Africa of the so-called Campagnie du Kassai, and with the present representative of the trading company, and the other against Dr. Sheppard.... The *Greffier*, or clerk, of the court, however, combined the two in one summons, charging Dr. Morrison as the responsible editor of the *Kassai Herald*.... Owing to this error in the drafting of the summons, the action against Dr. Morrison was withdrawn.[23]

Sheppard, along with Morrison, who was not aware that the charges had been dropped, was forced to travel close to a thousand miles from Luebo to Leopoldville to stand trial. The journey took over two months. Arriving at N'Gela, close to Leopoldville, Sheppard was told of a sick white man four miles outside the village. Apparently the natives refused to help him because, as Sheppard discovered, he had been an agent of the Kassai Company. Sheppard interrupted the journey to his trial for five days to remain and nurse the sick agent of the company suing him.[24]

The case received much publicity, especially in the United States, where Sheppard and Morrison generated support for their stand on human liberty, even for African natives. The Boston *Herald* said that "the case has attracted much international attention."[25] The U.S. government assigned William W. Handley, American consul-general, to witness and report on the proceedings. In his letter to the assistant secretary of state Handley noted that the trial was being conducted by representatives appointed by the Belgian government, which owned 50 percent of the Kassai Rubber Company stock and which appointed the directors of the company. Nevertheless, he noted that Sheppard and Morrison's legal counsel was M. Emile Vandervelde, whom Morrison described as "the great

Socialist leader in Belgium . . . who has stood almost alone in his country all these years in defence of the natives against the spoliation *regime* of King Leopold." Vandervelde traveled to the Congo and conducted Sheppard's defense without fee because of his support for the stand they took on behalf of the native workers. The case was heard by Judge Gianpetrie, an Italian apparently appointed by the Belgian parliament because of his impartiality.[26] In spite of this it appeared that Sheppard might not receive a fair hearing because the court would not allow him to introduce evidence to prove his accusations. He was nevertheless acquitted of the charges brought against him. The Kassai Company appealed his acquittal, but seemingly nothing further was done.[27]

Sheppard's acquittal was interpreted as a victory for the rights of African natives and also as a triumph for the Christian missionaries in Africa, many of whom felt compelled to champion the rights of the native workers whom they were trying to convert. In this, Sheppard led the way. The attitude of the commentator for the *Presbyterian Standard* was typical:

We hail this announcement [of acquittal] with joy, not only for the sake of the missionaries themselves, who are thus delivered from the horrors of a Congo prison . . . but especially for the sake of the poor Congo natives, for whom this triumph of justice means that the protest of the Christian world in their behalf has been loud enough and strong enough to defeat the wicked conspiracy of the rubber gatherers to drive out of the country those who refuse to be silent witnesses to the cruelties which were a necessary feature to the business they were carrying on if that business was to be made financially profitable.[28]

Another reporter called Sheppard the American Negro hero of the Congo, noting that "he was the first to stir the world with the tale of the Congo abuses." Subsequently the Congo Free State became a colony under the control of the Belgian parliament instead of the private preserve of King Leopold.[29]

In spite of his acquittal and a sense of the progress his protest had begun, Sheppard was broken in health from the long journey to Leopoldville and the strain of the trial.[30] Returning to the United States where he was in great demand as a lecturer, he became the pastor of Grace Presbyterian Church in

Louisville. In recognition of his achievements in Africa, he was also listed in *Who's Who in America,* a rare accomplishment for a Negro of this period.[31] Sheppard not only championed African rights but also established a successful mission. Although he worked in the Congo for five years before winning a single convert, by the time he left in 1910, there were 51 American missionaries in service, 457 native workers, 15,674 church members, 275 schools with 15,934 students, 3 theological schools training 160 natives for the ministry, 338 Sunday schools with 32,775 day students, and 938 native teachers.[32]

Why did Sheppard champion the natives against those, in both government and business, who would exploit them? There are three reasons. He felt that it was his duty as a missionary to improve the lives of his fellow men; he developed a deep interest in the African tribesmen; and he was guided by the philosophy of Hampton Institute. The first needs no discussion; the second and third do.

At least part of the answer can be found in Sheppard's developing attitude toward the Africans he was converting to Christianity, an attitude revealed in his moral tracts, addresses, and letters and in his account of his days in the Congo. In many of these works Sheppard repeated the same incidents—his early mission with Lapsley, his striving alone after Lapsley's death, his contact with the elusive Bakuba, his confrontation with the Zappo-Zaps, and his trial—but his basic conception of the African people and their culture gradually changed. Between 1893, when he delivered "Into the Heart of Africa," his first address on Africa, and 1917, when he published *Presbyterian Pioneers,* his account of the early days in the Congo, he learned to appreciate African culture.[33]

In addition to his letters, speeches, and book, Sheppard also published four moral tracts—*An African Daniel, A Little Robber Who Found a Great Treasure, The Story of a Girl Who Ate Her Mother,* and *A Young Hunter.*[34] These stories about Africans whom he "saved" further reveal his attitudes toward the natives and also toward the Belgian government which ran the Congo for King Leopold. They help one more fully to understand his concern for the rights of African natives. These stories of uncertain date all deal with his early experiences in the Congo and reflect his early attitudes.[35] The stories were written to teach American children about the great work being done in Africa, and three of the four stories feature children who became converts and carried the word of God and Jesus Christ to their people.

In his accounts of the early days, Sheppard, like Lapsley, felt apprehensive about the journey to Luebo and feared being attacked by unfriendly African natives. At Stanley Pool, however, after their long trek overland from Matadi, they seemed to be more relaxed about the natives. They had not been attacked on their long march, and the Bateke natives at Stanley Pool proved friendly. Perhaps because missionaries had already established a station there and because it was also the last major outpost and trading center on the Congo, the natives showed no hostility. But as they prepared to go overland into the interior to seek a suitable site for their mission, their initial fears appeared to be justified. Sheppard had to travel 140 miles through the bush to find native bearers from the Kinkunji tribe for their overland trek. Once back at Stanley Pool, the bearers disappeared into the bush because they feared an attack by the Kwango, a hostile tribe.[36] Sheppard and Lapsley then decided to travel on the river, first by canoe, then by steamer. As they journeyed deeper into the heart of Africa, they noted that the natives became increasingly hostile and they had some close calls; yet they managed to arrive at Luebo without actually being attacked. The Bakete tribesmen at Luebo offered no resistance to their settling there, although Sheppard did say that "they were afraid of us and we were afraid of them."[37]

Sheppard and Lapsley's fear moderated as they went about their work of educating and attempting to convert the Bakete. Some sense of cultural superiority and perhaps even a slightly negative feeling toward the people emerges from these early accounts. Commenting on his early emotions, especially after Lapsley had died and he was isolated from what he considered civilized society, Sheppard wrote that "the dense darkness of heathenism had depressed me," and referred to the Bakete as "the wild and barbarous tribe with which I am living." Sheppard's first response was conditioned by his Christian bias, not by the friendly and open treatment he received. Sheppard again called the Bakete "wild, naked savages, bowing down to idols, filled with superstition and sin."[38] This same attitude can be seen clearly in *A Young Hunter,* one of Sheppard's children's stories. In it Benwenya, the first Bakuba convert at Ibanj, is a hunter of game who becomes a hunter of the souls of men once he is converted from his native superstition and ignorance to the truth. In discussing Benwenya's mission of converting other Bakuba, Sheppard comments: "Hundreds of *poor blind wretched* native Africans have been converted to the religion of the Lord Jesus Christ because of this young man."[39]

It should be pointed out that Sheppard's early attitude toward the Africans was not unusual. For example, an anonymous article, "William Sheppard: Christian Fighter," praises Sheppard for his championing the rights of the Africans and for his attempts to free them from the control of the Kassai Rubber Company, but does so by derogating the natives: "He [Sheppard] had spoken in positive terms of the suffering which a subsidized rubber company had brought to the *simple-minded, almost helpless* African natives."[40] The African was viewed as a child who needed help from the missionaries.

Sheppard did not apply this standard of cultural and religious superiority just to the natives in Africa but also to Negroes and American Indians. He thought of Samuel Chapman Armstrong as an American missionary who "saw the mass of Negro men and women, *degraded, ignorant,* and *superstitious; poor,* without God and without a friend; lost, bowed down under a great burden." And he interpreted Armstrong's journey to the West to bring Indians back to Hampton Institute as a missionary's attempt to save the savages.[41] Sheppard applied the same opprobious terms to Africans, Negroes, and American Indians, indeed, to all who needed to be civilized by being Christianized.

Although he viewed the African natives generally as "ignorant" and "savage," he kept his most negative comments for the Zappo-Zaps, because he abhorred their cannibalism and their working for the Belgian officers to collect rubber quotas and taxes. They seemed to be both actual and metaphoric cannibals, feeding off the people body and soul. Sheppard called them "perhaps the lowest [tribe] in Africa."[42]

Again, in the story *A Little Robber*, he referred to them as "the horrid, blood-thirsty Zappo-Zaps who sharpen their teeth till they look like cross-cut saws and who eat the flesh of human beings." Another real-life cannibal story, *The Story of a Girl*, is about Ntumba, a child who ate her mother. Some of the Zappo-Zaps were on a forced march with their hostages, one of whom was Ntumba's mother, whose feet became so swollen that she could not continue. The cannibals killed her, and then they and Ntumba feasted on her. Lapsley bought the girl from the Zappo-Zaps and converted her. Although her conversion gratified them, on the whole they had little success among the Zappo-Zaps. Most of their converts were from the Bakete or Bakuba tribes.[43]

As we have seen, Sheppard and Lapsley both became quite interested in the Bakuba tribesmen whom they saw trading with the Bakete, and contact with this tribe caused Sheppard to revise some of his preconceptions about Africans, which had apparently been reinforced by the Bakete. Most of Sheppard's writings, talks, and even curios and handicrafts are about and from the Bakuba, with whom Sheppard lived for some time at Ibanj, where he and Lucy settled. At first, though fascinated by the seeming superiority of the Bakuba, he also felt an antipathy toward many of their superstitions and related customs. In *Presbyterian Pioneers* he made the point that he "was astounded to find a people in Central Africa so intelligent and yet so far from the truth," which suggests both his original bias that they were simple-minded and his commitment to Christian truth.[44]

Before entering Ibanj, Lukenga's capital, Sheppard carefully studied Bakuba customs, especially those superstitious beliefs pertinent to the administration of justice and the maintenance of social order. To the Bakuba no occurrence was natural, and therefore each event, even death, must be caused by a man. A person suspected of committing a crime or of causing a death was subjected to a "truth test," a torture appropriate to the suspected crime and harmless to the innocent. If accused of murder, a person would be given a lethal dose of poison. If the poison made him sick and he threw up, he would live and would therefore have been proved innocent. If, on the other hand, he died, then obviously he was guilty and so had been punished. If a person were accused, say, of stealing, his arm would be plunged into boiling water. If the skin were not scalded and did not peel off, he was innocent, but if he were scalded, he was judged guilty and fined. Girls suspected of stealing were subjected to a more painful ordeal than the men. The witch doctors would "put pepper in the girls' eyes and hold it tight with a copper wire and say, 'If you are not guilty it will not burn you.' I have seen a girl going around for weeks with sick and swollen eyes, and in their minds she was guilty." The Bakuba even applied this concept to severe weather. While Sheppard was first staying in Ibanj a tornado struck the city, causing minor damage. King Lukenga called Sheppard before him and asked him the reason for the violent storm. Sheppard, of course, professed ignorance of the cause, whereupon Lukenga suggested that his washing clothes in the stream caused the storm and advised him not to wash them again.[45] The Bakuba, exceedingly superstitious, always looked to human causes for natural phenomena.

As he lived with them, Sheppard began to admire the Bakuba as a people and changed his perception of them: "I grew very fond of the Bakuba and it was reciprocated. They were the finest looking race I had seen in Africa, dignified, graceful, courageous, honest, with an open smiling countenance and really hospitable. Their knowledge of weaving, embroidery, wood carving and smelting was the highest in equatorial Africa."[46] Sheppard championed the Bakuba because of their highly developed government, equitable system of justice, and artistic skills, all of which were threatened by the Zappo-Zaps and rubber companies. Sheppard, as a matter of fact, was so fond of them that he named his son Maxamalinge after one of King Lukenga's sons.[47]

Sheppard wrote the article in the *Kassai Herald* for which he was brought to trial to show how the system of enforced labor was changing the Bakuba by destroying their institutions and by giving them little time to do their own work. Phrases in this article document how much Sheppard's attitudes had changed: "great stalwart men and women, who have from time immemorial been free," "a government not to be despised," "these magnificent people," "prosperous and intelligent." Living with the Bakuba at Ibanj, Sheppard had grown to appreciate their African culture, customs, and art, although he still sought to impart western culture and religious values to them. As he developed an appreciation for their culture, he saw how important it was to help them preserve their way of life, especially their Christianity. For example, Sheppard helped Katembua, chief of a Bakuba village and, surprisingly, also a bugler in the Belgian army, whose story he tells in *An African Daniel*. After Katembua had been converted, he wanted to leave the army and spread the word of God to the natives, but the Belgians arrested him and sent him to Lusambo, three hundred miles away, a ten-day journey. When his arrest became known, the missionaries protested, saying "the world should hear of [the Belgians'] cruelty and their injustice."[48] Katembua was released from both jail and army.

Sheppard supported the Africans not only because he developed an interest in, and respect for, them but also because of the profound impact Hampton Institute had on him, a recurring theme in his letters, addresses, and other writings. Sheppard heard of Hampton Normal and Agricultural Institute, as the college was then called, while living in Covington, Virginia, where he was a headwaiter at a McCurdy House restaurant. He reported having "secured some literature from there and read carefully every word. I saved my money, and in 1880 said good-bye to my parents and was off to school." Sheppard attended night school in 1881–82, while he worked on the farm during his first year and at the bakery his second.[49] He was a junior in 1882–83, but never finished the term because he went to Stillman Institute, where he remained for three years. Although at Hampton Institute for only two years, Sheppard considered it the home of his spiritual birth.

In many of his writings he narrates two Hampton incidents, referring to them time and again. The first concerns the warm reception he received from Principal Armstrong when he arrived in 1881 without first having made application. Sheppard said: "General Armstrong was my ideal of manhood: his erect carriage, deep, penetrating eyes, pleasant smiles and kindly disposition drew all students to him. He was a great, tenderhearted father to us all."[50] This incident shows the inspiration that Sheppard drew from General Armstrong personally and suggests that Sheppard modeled himself after Armstrong, being "a great tender-hearted father" to the African tribesmen. The second event provided him with his life's mission:

One Sabbath, at the close of afternoon Sabbath school, Dr. Frissell [then chaplain at Hampton Institute] came to me and said, "We are going to a village near by to hold divine service: won't you bring along some Bibles and hymn books?" I was delighted. I happened to be the only student in the number and I was so impressed and inspired by that splendid missionary effort in Slabtown that on Monday afternoon I got permission to go back. . . . I saw the needs of my people. . . . This, through this great man's kindness and influence, was my first missionary work. Later it was the pleasure of my life to do more missionary work—twenty years' service in the Congo in Central Africa.[51]

Perhaps this mission to Slabtown made such a deep impression on him because of his earlier predilection for religious work. Sheppard noted that when he was a youth in Waynesboro, a white lady saw him and said that he would be a missionary one day.[52]

Dedicated to becoming a missionary, hoping to go to Africa, he had to leave Hampton Institute for Stillman, where he could receive the necessary theological training. But he maintained close and continual contact with his spiritual home, accounts of which fill his private and public papers. For example, while in the Congo in 1892 Sheppard received an inspirational letter from Armstrong that he often quoted: "We are praying for you, and we expect the story of Hampton to be told in the Congo valley."[53] Sheppard also kept in close contact by letter with Myrtilla J. Sherman, who had been his grammar instructor at Hampton, sending her such curios as an intricately carved wooden napkin ring. At Hampton Institute, on November 14, 1893, during his brief return to the United States, he presented "Into the Heart of Darkest Africa," a lecture about his initial missionary experiences at Luebo and Ibanj.[54] Further, in 1904 Sheppard sent a letter to the *Southern Workman* which provided additional insight into his relationship with Hampton Institute: "Every message from Hampton brings such sweet reminiscences of the happy, pleasant, and profitable years I spent

there. Like a dear mother she has been devoted to, interested
in, and thoughtful of me since my departure; so much so that I
feel unworthy of her great love and devotion. However I have
tried and do try very hard to live up to her standard of teaching. I have endeavored, too, to put in practice all the lessons,
spiritual, mental, and industrial, learned while there."⁵⁵ Much
of Sheppard's motivation was provided by trying to "live up to"
Hampton Institute.

Sheppard returned to Hampton in January 1915, when he
delivered two addresses, both of them on Founder's Day. "Give
Me Thine Hand" paid tribute to General Armstrong and Hollis
Burke Frissell; "Sheppard on Africa" described his experiences
as a missionary. In the latter Sheppard said: "I am glad to
return to Hampton, the place of my birth—not natural birth,
but the place where I was born in instruction and inspiration
and vision. It was here I learned to do the impossible. It was
here that I learned that there were no barriers, no mountains,
that with God all things are possible. It was here I did my first
missionary work."⁵⁶ And in "Give Me Thine Hand" Sheppard
exhorted the students to "live up to" the Hampton tradition by
helping others to help themselves.

Sheppard last visited Hampton in 1923, but no details of his
visit appear in the Sheppard Papers. Sheppard may have
presented additional materials for his African art collection
housed at the Blake Museum, Hampton Institute. During his
sojourn in Africa, Sheppard had collected many art objects and
curios, especially from King Lukenga of the Bakubas, over one
hundred fifty of which were purchased by the Blake
Museum.⁵⁷

In February 1911 Sheppard and Booker T. Washington attended Hampton Institute fund-raising efforts in New York
City on the seventh and in Boston on the eighth.⁵⁸ In New York
they both addressed the gathering of potential donors. Undoubtedly these famous Hamptonians aided the Hampton
cause in both New York and Boston. Interestingly enough,
Sheppard was mentioned in the headlines, "Congo Missionary
Addresses White and Black Audience," but Washington was
not.⁵⁹ In his New York City talk Washington discussed the
influence of Hampton's "education for life" philosophy on its

graduates. "Graduates of Hampton ... have established schools patterned after it all through the South, and the influence of Hampton, as shown by Dr. Sheppard's address, already has been felt in the heart of Africa."[60] When he founded Tuskegee Institute, Booker T. Washington continued the learning-by-doing philosophy of Hampton Institute. Similarly, in the mission schools at Ibanj and Luebo, Sheppard taught students such trades as carving chairs and printing books.

Both men personify the Hampton spirit. Sheppard was a pioneer in the Congo Free State where, in the tradition of Hampton, he helped others help themselves. He established outposts and schools at Luebo and Ibanj. He also spoke out for what was just. In the affair of the Zappo-Zaps, he saved lives and called attention to atrocities sanctioned by a civilized government. Later he exposed exploitation of the native workers by the Kassai Rubber Company. Regardless of danger or personal risk, Sheppard spoke out. He followed the advice he gave to the Hampton Institute student body in 1915: "Apply faithfully your hand, your heart, and your brain to all that is offered you."[61]

In his eulogy for Sheppard, William Aery, the editor of the *Southern Workman,* described the Hampton philosophy that helped make Sheppard a fighter for African rights as well as a dedicated missionary: "Hampton, through its many graduates and ex-students who have gone into service for others with a strong faith in God and in their fellow-men, has been preaching for over forty years the doctrine of intelligent, fearless, prayerful action in behalf of those who are oppressed or in darkness."[62]

Notes

1. Booker T. Washington and William H. Sheppard were acquainted while students at Hampton Institute. In "Cruelty in the Congo Country" Washington says of Sheppard: ". . . a colored missionary whom I knew slightly as a fellow-student at Hampton Institute" (*Outlook* 78 [1904], 377).

2. "William Sheppard: Christian Fighter for African Rights," *Southern Workman* 39 (1910), 9.

3. At this time the Congo Free State was a protectorate of King Leopold II of Belgium. This arrangement was established at the Berlin Conference, Sept. 15, 1884, in which fourteen powers, including the United States, took part. All fourteen powers ratified this agreement in 1885 ("The Congo Free State and Its Missions," *Missionary*, 1900, pp. 270–71, in Sheppard Papers, Archives, Hampton Institute, Hampton, Va.).

4. William H. Sheppard, *Presbyterian Pioneers in Congo* (Richmond, Va.: Richmond Press [1917]), p. 20.

5. "William H. Sheppard, on Africa, Cleveland Hall Chapel, January 31, 1915," an address delivered at Hampton Institute, Sheppard Papers. In *Presbyterian Pioneers* (pp. 46–47), Sheppard notes that before settling at Luebo, they made an earlier trip from Stanley Pool to the rapids of Mwamba on the Kassai River, which means "river of the spirits," because the natives thought that spirits of people eaten by crocodiles resided there. The rapids proved impassable; so they journeyed back about two hundred miles to Stanley Pool. Later they took the steamer *Florida* to Luebo, where they stayed and established their mission.

6. *Presbyterian Pioneers*, p. 81.

7. Sheppard and his men followed a group of Bakuba traders into the interior, staying well behind, since the way to Ibanj was secret, outsiders not being allowed to journey to it. Sheppard stayed in numerous villages along the way and learned much of the Bakuba people, their superstitions, customs, and laws. He stayed over a year in Ibanj (William H. Sheppard, "Into the Heart of Africa," *Southern Workman* 24 [1895], 66).

8. "A Missionary Heroine," *Central Presbyterian* (1906), in William H. Sheppard: American Negro Hero of Congo, Newspaper Clippings 1904–09, Peabody Room Clipping File, no. 79. Another newspaper article in this file, "Africa Turning to Christianity, Missionary Says," asserts that Sheppard "ranks second only to Livingstone and Stanley in the opening of Central Africa" (Richmond *Times-Dispatch*, Apr. 27, 1908).

9. Boston *Transcript* (1893), Peabody Room Clipping File, no. 79.

10. William H. Sheppard, "Light in Darkest Africa," *Southern Workman* 34 (1905), 220.

11. *Missionary*, 1900, p. 274, Sheppard Papers.

12. Letter, Sept. 13 and 14 [1899], Historical Foundation of the Presbyterian and Reformed Churches, Montreat, N.C.; copy in Sheppard Papers.

13. "Light in Darkest Africa," p. 220.

14. Letter, Sept. 13 and 14 [1899], Montreat; copy in Sheppard Papers.

15. "Light in Darkest Africa," p. 225.

16. Typical articles are: "The Congo Free State and Its Missions," *Missionary*, 1900, pp. 270–75; W. M. Morrison, "Africa between the Upper and the Nether Millstones," *Missionary*, 1900, pp. 61–63, Sheppard Papers.

17. Washington, "Cruelty," pp. 375–77. Washington stated that much of his information came from "a report written on the spot by an eye-witness. Mr. Sheppard had been sent out by the mission to investigate what is called a 'rubber raid'" (p. 377). The report referred to is most likely the one that

Sheppard sent to the Belgian authorities in 1899, which I have been unable to trace. The unaddressed September 13 and 14 letter of Sheppard (Montreat; Sheppard Papers) concerning this may actually have been a journal which he used as the basis for his report. The letter provides many more exact details than appear in his public comments.

18. "Personal Notes," *Southern Workman* 34 (1905), 127. The two autograph cards are in the Montreat Papers; copies in Sheppard Papers. Further presidential contact is suggested by a note dated August 5, 1924, from President Calvin Coolidge to Sheppard, thanking him for his condolences (Montreat; copies in Sheppard Papers).

19. D. J. Sanders, president of Biddle University, to William Sheppard, July 7, 1905, notifying him of his selection to receive the degree Doctor of Divinity, Sheppard Papers.

20. *Kassai Herald,* Luebo, Jan. 1, 1908; reprinted in "William Sheppard: Christian Fighter," pp. 8–9.

21. Ibid., p. 10.

22. Boston *Herald,* Oct. 17, 1909, Peabody Room Clipping File, no. 79; W. M. Morrison, "Some Phases of the Trial of Sheppard and Morrison," *Kassai Herald,* Luebo, Mar. 1, 1910, p. 8, Sheppard Papers.

23. "William Sheppard: Christian Fighter," pp. 9–10.

24. *Africo-American Presbyterian,* Feb. 17, 1910, Peabody Room Clipping File, no. 79.

25. Boston *Herald,* Oct. 17, 1909, ibid.

26. Handley to Assistant Secretary of State, Sept. 21, 1909, copy in Sheppard Papers; Morrison, "Some Phases," p. 8; "William Sheppard: Christian Fighter," p. 9.

27. Boston *Herald,* Oct. 17, 1909, Peabody Room Clipping File, no. 79.

28. Reprinted Charlotte, N.C., *Star of Zion,* 1909, ibid.

29. Boston *Herald,* Oct. 17, 1909, and Amsterdam *News,* March 13, no year, ibid.

30. W. A. Aery, "A Courageous Christian," *Southern Workman* 57 (1928), 62. Perhaps Sheppard caught fever from the Kassai Co. agent he nursed back to health. By 1905 Sheppard had had sixty-five bouts with African fever ("Light in Darkest Africa," p. 218).

31. Boston *Herald,* Oct. 17, 1909, Peabody Room Clipping file, no. 79.

32. *Presbyterian Pioneers,* p. 151. W. M. Morrison in *Story of Our Congo Missions* (Nashville, Tenn.: n.p., n.d.), p. 5, listed the following as Black missionaries to the Congo: 1894, Mrs. Sheppard, Rev. H. P. Hawkins of Mississippi, and the Misses Maria Fearing and Lillian M. Thomas of Alabama; 1895, Rev. J. E. Phipps.

33. "Into the Heart of Africa," pp. 182–87.

34. All of the tracts were published by Hampton Institute Press and have the subtitle *True African Stories.*

35. He first mentions the stories in his 1915 address "Sheppard on Africa," Sheppard Papers. This may suggest that, though possibly written earlier, they were published about 1915.

36. *Presbyterian Pioneers*, p. 42.

37. "Sheppard on Africa," Sheppard Papers.

38. William H. Sheppard, "Give Me Thine Hand," Founder's Day address, 1915, Hampton Institute, *Southern Workman* 44 (1915), 166, 169.

39. *A Young Hunter,* Sheppard Papers (italics mine).

40. "William Sheppard: Christian Fighter," p. 11 (italics mine).

41. "Give Me Thine Hand," p. 167 (italics mine).

42. "Light in Darkest Africa," p. 220.

43. *A Little Robber* and *The Story of a Little Girl,* Sheppard Papers.

44. *Presbyterian Pioneers*, p. 132.

45. "Sheppard on Africa," Sheppard Papers.

46. *Presbyterian Pionners,* p. 137.

47. Ibid., p. 115; "Sheppard Is Here," Amsterdam *News,* March 13, no year, Peabody Room Clipping File, no. 79. Sheppard had four children who were born in the Congo, two of whom survived. Wilhelmina, the other surviving child, took charge of the recreational activities of the girls at the Community House for Colored People in Hampton, thus keeping Sheppard's ties close to the Hampton community.

48. *An African Daniel,* p. 4, Sheppard Papers.

49. *Presbyterian Pioneers*, pp. 16–17.

50. Ibid., p. 17.

51. William H. Sheppard, "Unconscious Influence," *Southern Workman* 46 (1915), 590.

52. *Presbyterian Pioneers,* p. 16.

53. "Give Me Thine Hand," p. 168.

54. "Into the Heart of Africa," pp. 61–66.

55. William H. Sheppard, "The Bakuba Missions," *Southern Workman* 33 (1904), 408.

56. "Sheppard on Africa," Sheppard Papers. Sheppard's last honor was having a lake that he discovered in the Kassai district named Lake Sheppard ("Hampton Incidents," *Southern Workman* 44 [1915], 183).

57. "Hampton Incidents," *Southern Workman* 40 (1911), 448; William H. Sheppard, "African Handicrafts and Superstitions," ibid. 50 (1921) 401–8.

58. "Tells of Work with Negroes," New York *Press,* Feb. 8, 1911, and Boston *Transcript,* Feb. 9, 1911, Peabody Room Clipping File, no. 79.

59. New York *Press,* Feb. 8, 1911, p. 20, ibid.

60. "Tells of Work with Negroes," New York *Press,* Feb. 8, 1911, ibid.

61. "Give Me Thine Hand," p. 169.

62. From untitled two-page manuscript signed "Wm. Aery." on back, in Sheppard Papers. This manuscript seems to be a handwritten draft for "A Courageous Christian."

William Howard Taft and Hampton Institute

Howard V. Young, Jr.

WILLIAM HOWARD TAFT was elected to Hampton Institute's Board of Trustees in May 1909, almost at the very beginning of his presidency, and he continued a member of the Board until his death in March 1930. He remained very much on the national scene after the end of his presidential term in March 1913, when he became a professor of constitutional law at Yale University. Following the death of Robert C. Ogden, president of Hampton's Board of Trustees, in 1914 Taft became head of this body in which capacity he continued serving even after he was appointed chief justice of the United States in July 1921.

Because of his positions as president and chief justice he was unable to attend trustee meetings regularly during those years and his place was filled from 1924 to 1930 by Clarence H. Kelsey, second vice president of Hampton's Board, who was a personal friend of Taft's and president of the Title Guarantee and Trust Company of New York. But while he was president of the United States, Taft did attend a meeting of the Board of Trustees on November 20, 1909, and visited the campus again on June 9, 1912; as chief justice he attended annual meetings of the Board in 1922, 1923, and 1924. These meetings coincided with Hampton's Annual Anniversary days (graduation) when he spoke and personally presented the diplomas and certificates to the graduates. A slight stroke in 1924 and deteriorating health kept him from attending any more meetings at Hampton, but a special one was held at his home in Washington, D.C., on March 3, 1926, during the Massenburg Bill controversy.

I

Even before he accepted membership on the Hampton Board of Trustees, Taft had delivered two major addresses on behalf

From left: unidentified, William Howard Taft, Booker T. Washington, Andrew Carnegie

of the school—one at Plymouth Church, Brooklyn, on March 16, 1908, when he was still secretary of war in Theodore Roosevelt's administration and the other at Carnegie Hall on February 23, 1909, as president-elect of the United States. On most occasions when he came to Hampton, he addressed public meetings on campus, giving the belated Fiftieth Anniversary Address in May 1919 and making a pronouncement on the "Negro Problem" in January 1921. These local visits and speeches were reported in campus publications such as the *Southern Workman* and the *Hampton Student,* in the Newport News and Norfolk press, and frequently by the national newspapers. Taft used these occasions to set forth his philosophy about education at Hampton Institute and the role the school was expected to play in solving the race problem nationally.

In discussing the history of the relations of Black people to American society from Emancipation to the present, Taft showed considerable objectivity about what had happened to the political rights of Black Americans. He stated on several occasions to northern audiences as well as at Hampton Institute that the southern states had virtually nullified the Fifteenth Amendment, which had granted the vote to the Black man.[1] And he recognized the sufferings and humiliation to which Black people were often subjected.[2] As he said to the students on his second visit to the campus in June 1912:

I do not wish to say much this morning, but if I can arouse in you, my colored brothers, my friends, a feeling that there are a great many people in this country with white skins who take a deep interest in your welfare, who understand the burdens that you have to carry because of the unjust race prejudice and the unjust treatment you receive at times, so that you can bear the burden that you have to bear with an absence of that loneliness as if you could not bear it because there was no one to sympathize with you, I shall feel as though I had accomplished something.[3]

And he occasionally, spoke against the lynchings of Black people:

Of course, we all deplore an outbreak, every once in a while of lynching—that horrible exhibition of inhumanity of men, growing out, first, of race prejudice, and then out of the instinctive brutality of men. You cannot explain it in any other way, because when you come to discuss motives you are at a loss in the bestiality that prompts it. . . . we cannot charge it to a race or to a people. We charge it to a few who are not properly punished, I agree, but you must remember that in this age one of the great dangers of our society and community is the possibility of destruction that one viciously inclined man, or a few viciously inclined men, can work upon innocent people.[4]

But Taft never seemed to realize the depth of racist feeling in America as he always qualified these criticisms of America's treatment of its Black citizens with such as the following:

The world is growing more and more generous; each man on the whole is becoming more considerate. The one to whom the Negro may look for sympathy is the white man of the South, educated, intelligent, and understanding the needs of the country as a whole, who knows that the Negro is here to stay in millions, that he must form a large part of the industrial South, that he has shown by the four decades of growth since the war that he is capable of great develop-

ment, of great progress, and that he has made himself of great value
to the South. . . . I believe that good feeling between the better class of
white and colored men of the South is growing.[5]

Taft even used the American entry into World War I to
reiterate his faith that Blacks would be treated fairly once the
whites recognized their value to American society:

War is dreadful and everyone would avoid it who could, but it has
some phases that do help. One of them is the equality that it produces
between all the citizens of the country engaged in war. All have the
privilege of dying for their country. All have the same concern in saving their country. And so these young men and young women of
Hampton who have felt from time to time the sense of injustice that
comes from racial prejudice and racial feeling may well take to
themselves the feeling that now, with the country in danger, they
reach nearer and nearer that equality that the Declaration of Independence assured them, and that with the loyalty and service they will
render they will make their race more valued by their white brothers
and sisters than it ever was before.[6]

And when the race riots and lynchings of Black people broke
out with renewed force in 1919, he counseled patience and
hope and said that racism was the work of individuals and not
characteristic of white Americans generally:

But, my friends, we are struggling with a generation. We are going
upward. As you look back fifty years, you can see that we have made
great progress. You heard what Dr. Moton said, and there is no man
who knows better, that even the average white men in the South are
coming to see the great mistakes that have been made in dealing with
the Negroes in their communities. That progress is something we
should rejoice over. It is something that should instil [sic] patience
against injustice, the depth of which many of us have always felt, and
the depth of which is now being realized among those people with
whom the Negroes of the country must live—the white people of the
South—and from whom the Negroes may reasonably expect that
they will get justice. They are the ones who can be real friends of the
Negro. They are the ones who can appreciate the value of the Negro
as he makes himself more valuable, and they are the ones with whom
it is of the highest importance that he should live in amity. The
Southern leaders are realizing that they must do their part. In the
anti-lynching convention that is to be held in New York, leading

Southerners are to appear to testify to their detestation of lynching and their knowledge that they must take measures in the South to redeem the honor and the decency of that section, and stamp out that awful impeachment against the civilization of the South and the United States.[7]

In retrospect one may conclude that Taft was a better administrator than an executive in the sense that he carried out policies initiated by someone else. He amassed a splendid record of public service beginning in the Philippine Islands from 1900 to 1904 when, as governor, he carried out the transition from military to civilian government; then as secretary of war from 1904 to 1909 when he was given the responsibility of supervising the digging of the Panama Canal; and as chief justice of the United States from 1921 to 1930 when he was very active in getting Congress to authorize various reforms in judicial procedures. But as the president of the United States from 1909 to 1913 he was not successful in instituting new policies. One might conclude the same about his relations with Hampton Institute. His tenure as a member and then president of the Board of Trustees (1909– 30) was marked more by his efforts to increase the endowment of the school and to foster its smooth running on traditional lines than for any suggestion of a change in direction of its program.

Taft regarded himself as "the defender of conservative government and conservative institutions."[8] And this conservatism is reflected in the consistency of his views about American racism and Hampton Institute's educational role throughout his association of twenty-one years with the school. In several of his major addresses dealing with the South and the race question, he set forth in some detail the same views of the history of the period since the Civil War.

Taft roundly condemned slavery even before an audience of white Southerners, but he accepted for the most part the contemporary view of Reconstruction, which placed the blame for the South's postwar problems on Black and Carpetbagger dominance of its state governments.[9] He had an amazingly realistic view of the means by which white Southerners negated the voting rights of Black people, and he was at pains to assure white Southerners that the possibility of repealing the Fifteenth Amendment was "utterly impracticable." But he condoned this very restriction of the suffrage in order to "prevent entirely the possibility of a domination of Southern state, county, or municipal governments by an ignorant electorate, white or Black," so long as educational and property restrictions were applied equally to both races. This view was entirely consistent with Taft's general distrust of majority rule and his belief that the Supreme Court should act as a brake on democracy.[10]

Although he recognized in part the prejudice and discriminatory action to which Black people were subjected by American society, Taft hastened to allay supposed white fears that elimination of racism would lead to social equality between the races: "The fear that in some way or other a social equality between the races shall be enforced by law or brought about by political measures really has no foundation except in the imagination of those who fear such a result. The Federal Government has nothing to do with social equality. The war amendments do not declare in favor of social equality. . . . Social equality is something that grows out of voluntary concessions by the individuals forming society."[11] He stressed that the "wiser leaders of the Negroes therefore, never insist upon social equality or make it part of their program of progress."[12]

These remarks do not reflect much change from Taft's statement as president-elect in his Carnegie Hall speech ten years earlier: "Now I know that no man can think of the humiliation and the agony of spirit that the Negroes have to suffer in their struggle upward, when they encounter the race feeling and the injustices to which it leads. But it may help them, I hope it will, to give them stronger character, and there is a future before them that if they overcome these obstacles is well worth the effort."[13]

On at least one occasion the lynching of Black people was raised at the Board of Trustees meeting—on May 2, 1919, which was the commemoration of Hampton's semicentennial. Francis G. Peabody, who had written a history of the school entitled *Education for Life,* said that the Boston Hampton Committee wished to make a formal protest to President Wilson against lynchings, but he suggested the Trustees should make such a statement. After some discussion in which the point was made that the president has no authority in regard to lynching, a protest resolution was adopted.[14] One wonders whether it was Taft who raised the doubt about the role the chief executive could play in suppressing this barbarous custom. The Board also decided to send representatives from Hampton Institute to the anti-lynching meeting to be held the next week in New York City.

Taft always maintained that

the great hope of the Negro is in the friendship of the Southern whites, and that there is real and genuine interest in his improvement, educational and moral, among the many good people of the South, is manifest by the various activities in which the Southern white people are engaged to help him. The enemy of the Negro, as before the war, is the poor-white element. It is from them that the cruel mobs are recruited. They conduct the lynchings and are guilty of the cruelties growing out of race prejudice. The law is not enforced as it should be in the South. Indeed, it is not enforced as it should be in the North, as we know to our humiliation; and everywhere we must restrain mob rule. In the South it is particularly directed against the Negro.[15]

Along with the rejection of the idea of repealing the Fifteenth Amendment, Taft also summarily dismissed the idea of the expatriation of American Blacks to Africa:

To me such a proposition is utterly fatuous. The Negro is essential to the South in order that it may have proper labor. An attempt of Negroes to migrate from one state to another not many years ago led to open violence at white instigation to prevent it. More than this, the Negroes have now reached 9,000,000 in number. Their ancestors were brought here against their will. They have no country but this. They know no flag but ours. They wish to live under it, and are willing to die for it. They are Americans. They are part of our people and are entitled to our every effort to make them worthy of their responsibilities as free men and as citizens.[16]

And "whenever called upon, the Negro has never failed to make sacrifices for this, the only country he has, and the only flag he loves." They have a right to expect, and do expect, not contumely and insult but gratitude for their services. However,

Negroes can mitigate "these injustices and bitter experiences" and "minimize them much in their pursuit of happiness."[17]

Taft believed fervently that social betterment of people resulted primarily from the automatic working of natural forces and without governmental interference, and he had total faith in the solution to racism embodied in the Hampton Institute creed of Samuel Chapman Armstrong and Booker T. Washington.[18] Progress would not come through legislation but through the economic success of Black people. Through the type of industrial and character training given at Hampton Institute "and its daughter, Tuskegee," the Blacks would gradually gain the respect of the better class of southern whites and would eventually be admitted to political participation.[19] "The better workmen they become, the better businessmen they become, the more they save, the more they accumulate, the better education they secure, the greater moral fibre they produce in their own characters, the more indispensable they will be in the communities in which they live. In doing so, they will create a motive on the part of the whites to accord them greater and greater consideration and more and more of their legal rights."[20]

Hampton Institute's plan of education was so vital to the success of Taft's solution that he held that "the founding of Hampton Institute constituted truly and historically an epoch in the development of the whole Negro race. Seldom can such a thing be truly said of the founding of any educational institution. To know the national and historical importance of Hampton, one must keep in touch with the educational movements through the South, and be able to distinguish between those which are in the line of real progress and those which are merely adjuncts and ancillary." Further, he sketched out his vision of the future course of race relations:

Now, what power has the industrial education at Hampton and Tuskegee, and the other institutions, upon this political phase of the Negro problem? It has the most direct effect in this, that the true basis of political influence in any community is industrial independence. This I understand to be the shibboleth of those who hearken to the teachings of Hampton and Tuskegee. If the Negro will make himself indispensable to the business prosperity of the South, his political influence will take care of itself. By education and the acquisition of property he will become a member of the community whose political influence, instead of being unlawfully destroyed, will be welcomed and encouraged. As the colored man becomes eligible under the laws imposing educational and property qualifications, his standing in the community will give weight to the vote he casts, and it is inevitable that in the end industrial success will bring him full political rights. But few maintain that the Negro today has not in the South an equal chance for bettering his condition by industry and education. The demand for labor with the increased prosperity of the South makes him more and more valuable to that section, and if by industrial education under the influence of the greatest of these great industrial institutions his usefulness as a member of the community has increased, race prejudice will fade before business necessity, and we shall have a rapidly growing Negro electorate in the South, whose political influence will be recognized in the States of the South as worthy of respect and as one to be reckoned with.[21]

Taft reverted to this theme in every successive address on the future of Blacks as he did when he told the candidates for certificates and diplomas at Hampton on April 27, 1915, that "Hampton is the center of an educational movement . . . that makes Hampton the most conspicuous and most important institution of learning we have in the country today . . . because this institution was aimed at the problem of bringing back into a life of freedom, five, six, ten millions of people who have been subjected to slavery."[22]

Believing that the solution to the racial problem depended on Southern whites, he tried to make them realize the value of an educated, diligent, Black working class. "The Negro is absolutely essential to the development of the South. His labor the South needs, and the more you instruct that labor the more valuable the Negro becomes to the South. Hence it is that the work of Hampton Institute has its intrinsic importance. It is the solution of the race question."[23] He was reiterating the same optimistic point he had made in more personal terms a year earlier.

We believe that the solution of the race question in the South is largely a matter of industrial and thorough education. We believe that the best friend that the Southern Negro can have is the Southern white man, and that the growing interest which the Southern white man is taking in the development of the Negro is one of the most encouraging reasons for believing the problem is capable of solution. The hope of the Southern Negro is in teaching him how to be a good farmer, how to be a good mechanic; in teaching him how to make his home attractive and how to live more comfortably and according to the rules of health and morality.[24]

Taft often pleaded with the South to believe that the North and the Republican Party did not mean to upset the political or social status quo in the South but merely wanted to obliterate sectional misunderstanding and mutually solve the race question.

On the eve of his inauguration as president of the United States he stated:

The recent election has made it probable that I shall become more or less responsible for the policy of the next Presidential Administration, and I improve this opportunity to say that nothing would give me greater pride, because nothing would give me more claim to the gratitude of my fellow-citizens, than if I could so direct that policy in respect to the Southern States as to convince its intelligent citizens of the desire of the Administration to aid them in working out satisfactorily the serious problems before them and of bringing them and their Northern fellow-citizens closer and closer in sympathy and point of view. During the last decade, in common with all lovers of our country, I have watched with delight and thanksgiving the bond of union between the two sections grow firmer. I pray that it may be given to me to strengthen this movement, to obliterate all sectional lines, and leave nothing of difference between the North and the South, save a friendly emulation for the benefit of our common country.[25]

Taft did not favor the movement of southern Blacks to the northern cities because, although it might temporarily have the effect of warning the South that "the Negroes had acquired an independence sufficient to migrate when conditions were objectionable," it had demoralizing effects on the urbanized Blacks in the long run.[26]

It was fundamental to Taft's thinking that the Blacks were a backward race that had made excellent progress since Emancipation but had not yet caught up with the whites and that "the South is the real home of the average Negro and agriculture and rural trades are the pursuits to which he seems best adapted." But the average Black had to be taught to be moral and to work hard:

> He is a happy, emotional, forgiving person. The influence of his dependence on others in slavery days he has not entirely thrown off, and he perhaps lacks, because of this ancestral trait, the independence and initiative of the white man. He is capable of being educated in these. Mere literacy and intellectual training do not of course suffice to make the Negro what he should be. There must grow and be implanted in him moral forces as well as the training of his intellect, but moral strength is a matter of slower growth. This is really the great problem in both races but it is more difficult with the Negroes than with the whites because of the difference in their origin and history. Economic progress is strong evidence of growing moral force, and the Negro has made real advance along this line.[27]

Taft's vision was optimistic, but his response was stereotypical. He envisioned political progress but thought it had to be based on economic progress.

> With the natural tendencies of the Negro, with his natural desire to be a farmer, with land easily within his reach, with the economic freedom that he has, with great opportunity for mechanical trades in country surroundings, with a definite goal before him, undisturbed by social theories, unaffected by political change or disturbance, taught that the labor of his hand is the most honorable thing that he can do, there is not anything that he cannot accomplish for his people by increasing their wealth and their economic importance, which are stepping-stones to the other rights to which they aspire.[28]

He constantly recurred to the theme that the average Black had to be taught the necessity and value of hard labor so that once he had achieved equality of opportunity, he might have the character, self-sacrifice, and foresight to improve upon that opportunity.[29] This was necessary because of the post-Emancipation experience of the Blacks when the newly enfranchised people "had somehow gotten it into their heads that freedom brought freedom from the necessity of labor and that work was an accompaniment of bondage."[30]

When Taft used the phrase "industrial education," he evidently meant learning how to become proficient at farming, homemaking, and the associated rural crafts and trades—not how to be factory workers or supervisors. So Hampton Institute was to teach not only the skills of these occupations but the dignity of labor. Taft even joined President Eliot of Harvard in wishing to establish vocational schools in every state and every community in the nation.[31]

Taft's highly materialistic view of life was basically that of the majority of contemporary Americans, who measured success by means of the work which enabled one to achieve "material independence," which in turn supposedly brought the respect of the community.[32] This attitude was forcefully illustrated in his talk to the Hampton students at the April 1921 Anniversary Exercises. Taft was obviously very disturbed by the opening remarks of Nannie Burroughs, principal of the National Training School of Washington, D.C., who asked, referring to the real purpose of the school, "What is the meaning of this?" As important as it was to have a fine physical plant and education in the use of the equipment and machinery, she concluded that Hampton stood for higher goals, such as "manhood, for character and service," which the teachers have been working all these years to instill in its graduates. To make her point clear she stated: "I am talking about getting ideals through people. We are living in a time when people stress the value of material things. We have gotten to think that people must have something or own something, that it is the material thing that counts. Hampton is trying to teach you that it is not the material thing that counts. It is not what you have, but what you are, that counts."[33] Such heresy evoked an immediate response from Taft, who, speaking as president of the Board of Trustees and chief justice of the United States, directed his comments toward a refutation of such idealism. Under the guise of completing the total picture of Hampton's goals, he said:

I am sure that Miss Burroughs, in depicting the ideal, the moral character, did not intend to minimize the importance of your success in making yourselves independent and able to support yourselves. While she properly holds material success as far less important in the ultimate triumph of life and the pursuit of happiness, she would, I am sure, be the last in any way to depreciate the importance of your winning success material to the extent of being independent, of being above and beyond debt, of being able to educate your children, to maintain yourselves, and to practice thrift.

If you wish to be materially successful—and I speak from a very considerable knowledge of the world, a very considerable knowledge of things as they are—assuming the education that you have had at Hampton, the necessity for constant, hard, tenacious labor is the chief element in your winning mateial success. Drudgery you may call it, but there are few successful men who cannot look back to a period in their lives when their work at the time seemed to them nothing but drudgery. . . . [the graduate] will have achieved material independence and will also have put himself in a position where he can make himself useful to his community, useful to his race, and a real unit among citizens, because it is the individuals, after all, that make up the nation. We cannot all be good by machine. It is all custom work, this matter of character. It is all hand work, and there is no machine business about it.[34]

II

Taft evidently became interested in Hampton through serving with Booker T. Washington, Hampton's most renowned alumnus up to that time, on the Jeanes Fund Committee. He was enlisted to speak on behalf of Hampton Institute at Plymouth Church, Brooklyn, on March 16, 1908, and was even willing to cut short his postelection vacation in Augusta, Georgia, to speak again in aid of the school at Carnegie Hall on February 23, 1909. While he was president of the United States, he managed to come to Hampton twice—once on November 20, 1909, after attending the final exercises of the Deeper Waterways Association in Norfolk on the preceding day. On Saturday morning, November 20, the chief executive left the presidential yacht, *Mayflower,* anchored off Old Point and came to the school in a launch in real Republican simplicity accompanied only by his military and civilian private secretaries, an official messenger, two Secret Service agents, and the five members of the Hampton welcoming committee. The president toured the trade school and the farm where students were at work on their usual jobs. He then attended the trustees' meeting and a noon luncheon. At 2:00 P.M. he appeared on the Mansion House porch and all the Hampton officers, teachers, and workers with their families were presented in turn to him. And at 2:30 P.M. the party moved to a public meeting in the gymnasium, where the president gave a short talk, "Hampton's Relation to Race Problems." Several other distinguished guests were called upon for their remarks, including Charles W. Eliot, president emeritus of Harvard University, former Governor Andrew Jackson Montague of Virginia, Andrew Carnegie, and five Hampton alumni. John D. Rockefeller, Jr., the British ambassador, Sir Horace Plunkett, and other distinguished philanthropists and educators were also present as guests of the school. All the speakers sounded a note of optimism about the betterment of race relations and joined Taft and Eliot in heaping praise upon Hampton's unique system of education, calling it the first major reform in American education in several hundred years and calling for the establishment of similar "Armstrong Institutes" for children of all races throughout the United States.[35]

President Taft's next visit to Hampton, on Sunday, June 9, 1912, was a briefer and more informal one. Having come down from Washington overnight on the *Mayflower,* he and his wife had breakfast in the school dining room while the Hampton choir sang "plantation songs." The party then inspected the school battalion and attended services in Memorial Church, where the president spoke words of sympathy and encouragement in the face of American racism to the students and waxed optimistic that

the world is growing more and more generous. Each man on the whole is becoming more and more considerate. The one to whom we may look for sympathy and help is the white man of the South, educated, intelligent and more understanding of the needs of the country as a whole; who knows that the Negro is here to stay in the millions, that he must form part of the industrial South, that he has shown by the four decades of growth since the war that he is capable of great progress, and that he has made himself of great value to the South, and he has in him the elements of making himself much more valuable to the South. I believe that good feeling between the better class of white and colored men of the South is growing.[36]

He also expressed the belief that even General Armstrong did not realize "the tremendous force that this institution which he founded was to exert in the history of this, our country, and in the solution of the difficulties, which for years have seemed insoluble."[37] Then, accompanied by the Frissells, the presidential party boarded the yacht *Sylph* for a trip up the James to visit Lower Brandon Plantation, returning to Old Point late Sunday evening when the *Mayflower* immediately started its return trip to Washington.[38]

Although Taft was able to attend only one trustee meeting while he was president, there was an active correspondence between Principal Frissell and him running to about one hundred fifty letters and telegrams which are now in the Library of Congress and the Hampton Archives. Frissell asked President Taft on several occasions (June 14 and December 23, 1909, December 3, 1910, and June 1, 1911) to speak at what were called "parlour meetings" in wealthy philanthropists' homes either in Washington or along the north shore of Massachusetts Bay, where Taft vacationed in the summer, as well as at public meetings in Washington, D.C. (January 31, 1912, and January 7, 1913). The purpose of these meetings was not only to raise money on behalf of the school but "to arouse belief in the Negro race" and to form "right public sentiment on this race question."[39] Taft good naturedly participated in most of these programs but occasionally the press of official business prevented his attendance. It is really a measure of his intense belief in the mission of Hampton's "industrial education" in solving the American racial situation that the president of the United States would condescend to appear at one of these parlour meetings even in Washington, D.C.

President Taft also assisted in raising money for Hampton by writing letters at Frissell's suggestion to wealthy businessmen such as Andrew Carnegie and his wife, whom Taft invited to join him on his tour of Norfolk and Hampton November 19–

20, 1909, and from whom Taft solicited an increased dona-tion.[40] Taft also allowed Hampton to make reference to the ways he was supporting the school, including a personal gift of $500 in 1910 as part of Frissell's money-raising efforts. The principal also asked Taft to request influential men like Robert Bacon of Chicago to serve on the Board of Trustees and to im-press on him especially "the importance of this work."[41] Frissell even requested Taft to continue the postmaster at Hampton Institute, and the president referred the letter the next day to the postmaster general.[42] On another occasion Frissell gave a letter of recommendation to a southerner to gain entree to President Taft when he visited Washington because "he is interested in the value of industrial education for the Negro."[43]

But beyond these direct concerns for the college, Frissell did not hesitate to ask President Taft to consider other matters. For instance, he wrote Taft in early April 1911 to recommend the appointment of J. Watson Allen of Boston to the Board of In-dian Commissioners and again in late November 1911 to in-tervene with the Post Office Department so that Irwin Martin, a Black mail carrier in New York City, could get leave to do some musical work. The president found upon inquiry that Martin had not even applied for the leave himself.[44] Frissell also asked Taft (May 29, 1912) to write the president of Howard University's Board of Trustees in favor of Dr. Thomas Jones, who had worked at Hampton, becoming president of that university. Taft did write Mr. Justice Barnard about this on May 29, 1912.[45] And Frissell requested that Taft be sure three well-informed people, whom he named, were put on the program to speak before the Conference of State Governors in December 1912 about the vital subject of agricultural credit. Taft arranged this on November 30th.[46]

The president appointed Daniel Smiley, at Frissell's behest, to the Board of Indian Commissioners on December 18, 1912 but was unable to do anything about restoration of the yearly government grant for educating Indians at Hampton, which was cut off by Congressman John H. Stephens of Texas, chairman of the Subcommittee on Indian Affairs. On December 19, 1912, Frissell even asked Taft to speak with Secretary of State Knox about getting extraterritorial status for the vocational school at Thessalonica, Greece, of which Frissell was a Board member; but evidently due to the Balkan wars the situation was too confused for American influence to attempt any such action.[47]

Certainly the high point of Hampton's influence in the federal government was reached during the administrations of Roosevelt and particularly of Taft, but Taft's retirement from public office in March 1913 actually enabled him to be much more personally involved in Hampton's affairs. The president of the Board of Trustees, Robert C. Ogden, who had been the partner of General Armstrong in directing Hampton's program along vocational lines, died August 6, 1913, and Taft, evidently through the influence of Clarence H. Kelsey, second vice president of the Board, accepted election in his place as Hampton's Board president on April 23, 1914. Taft became a professor of constitutional law at Yale University, but this involved an enormous reduction in his income from $75,000 a year as president of the United States (with an additional $25,-000 expense account) to $5,000 as a professor, so he was forced to economize, even though he did earn some extra money from lecture tours. He even began to accept reimbursement for his expenses when he attended Board meetings at Hampton at about $43.50 for the round trip from New Haven.[48] He accepted the presidency of Hampton's board with the understanding that his professional duties and extensive speaking engagements precluded him from attending more than one meeting a year. He lived up to this agreement by coming to the annual trustee meeting at Hampton from 1914 through 1922 (except for 1917 when he attended a special meeting in New York later in the year to select a successor to Frissell, who had died in August 1917).

Because of his financial situation and his own teaching and lecturing schedule, Taft had to decline invitations by Frissell to speak at meetings sponsored by Hampton. But the principal still often asked him to write to various influential men like Ford, Frick, and Eastman to influence them in favor of Hampton. But Taft doubted he would get anywhere with the last two.[49] The principal on several occasions still asked Taft to use his political influence against a proposed immigration bill that would have excluded all persons of African descent from coming into the United States, and against an estate-tax bill that would have taxed donations to educational institutions. But both these situations resolved themselves apparently without any interference from Taft.[50] Frissell was a member of the Board of the Colonization Society of New York and he asked Taft for his legal opinion on the purposes for which the various endowment funds could be used in Liberia. Taft replied that the endowment funds should not be used to establish vocational educational schools on the Hampton pattern.[51] Frissell was also very concerned about rumored plans of Britain and France to take over the Republic of Liberia under the pretext that it was being used as a base by German agents. After consulting the State Department, Taft was able to assure Frissell that the Allies had no intention of using the alleged breaches of Liberian neutrality as pretext for taking over the country, although he believed the country was really "over-run with Germans."[52]

Taft was probably of much greater use to the school in helping to ward off encroachments on its land by the federal government. In the spring of 1915 the quartermaster general desired to purchase eight acres of Hampton's farmland to use for expansion of the National Cemetery. The Board of Trustees opposed this sale, and Taft agreed to take the matter up at once.[53] The quartermaster general wrote Taft in July 1915 that the army would drop the matter and utilize space next to walks and roads for burials for the next five or six years.[54] Upon receipt of this decision, Taft wrote triumphantly to Frissell from has Canadian vacation retreat on July 13, 1915: "We have stopped the United States from taking our land— for a time at any rate, as you will see by the enclosed letter. I don't think they will disturb us during your time or mine."

But there were continual problems with military encroachments on Hampton's property during the war. The school sold seventeen acres of its farmland at Shellbanks farm in late 1916 to the government for use as an aviation training school, which became the nucleus of Langley Field; but the army commander cut down a large part of the Shellbanks woodland still owned by the college and used the timber "through some misunderstanding."⁵⁵ Then the military laid a pipeline through Shellbanks Farm to bring water to the base from Bethel Reservoir, all without asking the school's permission, and Hampton's protests were unheeded. Even at the end of World War I, the government decided to lay a spur track from the Chesapeake and Ohio Railroad line to Fort Monroe across the southern part of Whipple Farm in order to bring wounded soldiers more expeditiously from Newport News to the newly commissioned army hospital at the old soldier's home in Kecoughtan. The Executive Committee of the Board objected and said it would claim $7,500 damages from the government, but the spur was built anyway, along with train sheds and other service buildings along the right of way.⁵⁶

After much correspondence, early in 1920 the government board of appraisers offered to pay the paltry sum of $50 damages for the four acres north of the railroad spur, $33.33 for damage to land south of the spur, and $53.90 for rental of the land from January 1, 1919, to December 1, 1919, and $4.90 per month thereafter. But this rather insulting offer was summarily rejected by the school's Trustees on February 2, 1920. In January 1921 the Washington law firm representing Hampton said that even a new offer of $3,000 for damages to Shellbanks Farm and $1,400 for the railroad right of way was not enough, especially as the government in violation of its promise had not yet removed the now disused spur track across Whipple Farm as their contractor had disappeared. The government finally asked Hampton Institute itself to complete the work of removing the roadbed for $2,000.⁵⁷ The Board at its April 1920 meeting attempted to use Taft's political influence by appointing him a committee of one to interview Secretary of War Baker, but evidently the former Republican president had no political clout with a Democratic administration. Finally on June 17, 1921, a special Board meeting authorized its president, Taft, and second vice president, Clarence H. Kelsey, to settle the schools' claims. With a Republican administration back in office, the War Department Claims Board awarded $3,000 for damage to Shellbanks Farm and $2,614 for damages caused by the spur track through the Whipple Farm, this latter figure being double the original offer to say nothing of the absurd 1920 offer totaling $196.03. In addition the school was paid $180 a year in rental for the pipeline at Shellbanks Farm.[58]

The volume and cordiality of Taft's correspondence with Hampton's principal did not diminish with the passing of Frissell. The Taft papers in the Library of Congress contain about 250 letters which he exchanged between 1918 and 1930 with James E. Gregg, Frissell's successor. Taft attended one meeting of the Trustees at Hampton Institute every year after he retired from the presidency, and even after he achieved his life's ambition by being appointed chief justice of the United States by President Harding on June 30, 1921, he still came for the Anniversary days in 1922 and 1923. After he suffered a mild heart attack in February 1924, he did not attend any more Board meetings. However, Gregg and other trustees did visit him in Washington, and during the crisis over the Massenburg Bill in March 1926 a committee of the Board of Trustees met formally with the chief justice at his home. On several occasions Taft expressed the view that it would be better for the school to select a new president of the Board of Trustees, but Gregg assured him each time, as did the Board itself on occasion, that they all wished him to continue in that post.[59]

Gregg frequently wrote Taft about the choice of speakers for Founder's Day or for the Anniversary days in April and some-times asked him as president of Hampton's Trustees to add a written invitation of his own to that of the school. Gregg also so-licited a foreword from Taft for the forthcoming bulletin of the U.S. Office of Education about the history and work of Hampton Institute. In this same letter, Gregg put in a plea that Taft use his influence with President-elect Harding to keep John Claxton as U.S. Commissioner of Education: "He is a liberal minded Southerner; and a man of this sort, we feel, can often be more serviceable to Negro education than many a Northerner whose theories might seem broader but who would find more difficulty in putting them into practice in this part of the world." The principal even solicited Taft on occasion for a monetary contribution, as in his letter of February 28, 1921, when he asked Taft to join with other trustees in making a contribution ($100 to $250 was expected) to pay for distribution to influential people of Robert R. Morton's recently published autobiography.[60]

Gregg was quick to side with Taft when he aroused some adverse comment in Black circles because of the editorials he had recently written on the subject of the "Negro in Politics" for various newspapers like the Philadelphia *Public Ledger* in early 1921. Taft expressed his usual conservative view that the new Republican administration of President Harding should not unduly antagonize the South by appointing Blacks to office in that area but should confine such appointments to the District of Columbia and the North.[61] Groups like the Inter-Racial Committee of Philadelphia also took to the literary hustings and sometimes wrote extensive refutations of Taft's conservative approach to the achievement of Negro rights. They pointed out that although there was some evidence that "there is gradually dawning in the South a better social conscience," such enlightened Southerners were still "a powerless minority" in stopping such gross violations of Black rights as occurred in the frequent lynchings and almost total disfranchisement of the Black people at the polls.[62]

Taft's view of his editorials was that although they "have been criticised and hammered by my negro fellow citizens, . . . I am telling them the truth, and their newspaper editors and their orators, as distinguished from their real leaders, have not learned yet to accept the truth." Gregg commiserated with him because of "the recent unfair criticisms of you in which some of the colored editors and professional politicians have indulged," and he used this incident to try to get Taft to come down to Hampton's Anniversary Day so that it would be made plain that "Hampton Institute is backing you, believes in you to the limit and is able to distinguish between the true and the pretended friends of the colored race."[63]

Gregg had initially tried to reassure Taft of his support by printing his address (at Founder's Day, January 1921) in full in the *Southern Workman* "so that everything you say might have its proper context and chances for misunderstanding be correspondingly reduced. Only one critical letter has come to me about it, and that from a man who is known as a habitual objector." Later Gregg expressed himself more fully on Black criticism of those whites who were associated with Black causes: "I suppose that it is part of the youthfulness and concomitant crudity of the Negro Americans—of some of them at least—to turn on their best friends with unwarranted denunciation. General Armstrong experienced it and so did Booker Washington, and so did Dr. Frissell. Dr. Moton is getting his share and I suppose that my turn will come some day. I trust that the wiser heads may soon perceive the utter unfairness of the criticisms which have been directed against you."[64]

Many times Taft was unable to fulfill requests from either Gregg or, infrequently, the Board of Trustees, as when he joined Gregg in urging President Harding to stop at Hampton Institute when he was to review the U.S. fleet in Hampton Roads, May 1921.[65] Gregg met at the White House with President Coolidge seven years later and tried to have him consent to participate in Hampton's sixtieth anniversary celebration in April 1928. Taft also tried to use his influence on the president but had to report: "I am very sorry that the President is not able to go to Hampton, but I am not surprised. He had disappointed me several times, but a man who has so much to do as he has is to be dealt with considerately—He makes a mistake in not going."[66] Nor did Taft have any better luck in inducing former Prime Minister Lloyd George to visit Hampton during his 1923 trip to the United States, although the chief justice wrote him that "Hampton Institute was in many respects the most important educational instrument in the solution of our political problems. . . . Hampton is her [Tuskegee's] mother and is in my judgment the hope of the race, and makes much for the solution of our race problem. I am perfectly delighted at the warmth of your reception by the American people. It shows they realize how much you did for the World in winning the War."[67]

One of Taft's greatest contributions to the school was made in connection with the very ambitious Hampton Institute–Tuskegee Institute Endowment Fund Drive during 1925. The chief justice was a great partisan on behalf of Hampton Institute, and in looking forward to these fund-raising efforts, he had written Gregg in a rather uncharacteristic vein that "it renders me impatient to think of the failure of those who are interested in the Carnegie and Rockefeller Foundations to appreciate the difference in canvassing for money for negro institutions and for those that have a rich constituency. It savors of the kind of narrow business rules to apply to everybody and everything which comes from too much business organization.[68] Taft participated actively throughout the drive, which involved chiefly getting matching funds to cover Eastman's conditional three-million-dollar pledge. Taft actively recruited key men to be the area chairmen for such cities as Washington, Detroit, Springfield, and Vicksburg.[69] He kept close track of the campaign's progress and in February 1925 warmly congratulated Gregg on securing $1,000,000 from John D. Rockefeller, Jr. It is interesting that in making his offer, Rockefeller should write to Gregg:

Inasmuch as I have been profoundly interested in these schools ever since my father took me as a small boy to visit Hampton when General Armstrong was its head, because they provide an education which fits boys and girls to be useful citizens, whether they go forward to higher and professional education or go directly into agriculture, industry or business, because they stress the development of character along with the development of mind and body and because of my lifelong interest in the colored race. . . .[70]

Although ill health prevented his attending a fund-raising luncheon meeting in New York in February 1925, Taft made a short speech during the intermission at the Hampton-Tuskegee concert in Carnegie Hall in late March; he even presided at a meeting held in the Hammonds' home in Washington on April 2, 1925.[71] When a member of the Southern Advisory Committee of the endowment campaign, Richard Manning of Columbia, South Carolina, raised questions about the teaching and practice of racial equality at the school,[72] Taft loyally supported Hampton and recommended that the principal's answer to Manning

should be carefully drawn so as to give the exact facts and not give the correspondent an opportunity to publish improper and unfounded inferences. From what I know, I should think the situation at Hampton was as free from the danger of promoting so-called miscegenation as any school of the kind could possibly be made so as not to injure the sensibilities of your students and friends. . . . I don't suppose you have any instruction on this subject [the social equality of the races]. The only equality that is taught is the political equality of the races and equality before the law in accord with the provisions of the 14th and 15th Amendments.[73]

This was among the first rumblings of the racial storm that broke over Hampton Institute in the spring of 1926 with the enactment of the Massenburg Law. Gregg in a letter to Taft, September 3, attributed the controversy's origin to Mrs. W. S. Copeland, wife of the editor of the *Daily Press* of Newport News, "who had come late to a crowded concert last winter and was angry because she had to sit nearer than she liked to colored people."[74] This had resulted in a *Daily Press* editorial on March 15 entitled "Integrity of the Anglo-Saxon Race," embodying a warning against the danger of amalgamation between the white and Negro races and charging Hampton Institute through a series of questions with the following crimes:

Do not the officers and teachers of the institution, white and colored, meet upon terms of social equality? And do not white teachers and colored pupils meet upon such terms?

Do not they on occasion sit together at the same table and have a sociable meal together without racial distinction?

Are not the students of Hampton Institute taught that the Negro race is in all respects the equal of the white race and that no racial distinctions should be made either in law or society?[75]

Hampton Institute might have escaped any serious consequences of the Copelands' displeasure had not a sort of housebroken Ku Klux Klan organization called the Anglo-Saxon Clubs of America taken up the cudgels. Its president, John Powell, a noted Virginia pianist, had just returned triumphantly to Richmond in July 1925 from an appearance before the Georgia legislature, where he had successfully urged them to enact "a radical race integrity law." As a result of a meeting of the Richmond Anglo-Saxon post on July 14, letters were sent to the twenty-two prominent Southerners, including the governors of Virginia and North Carolina, who were serving as members of the Hampton-Tuskegee endowment fund committee urging them to resign because "the Normal school was teaching and practising social equality between the races."[76] Fortunately none of these men did retire although several sent letters to Gregg requesting clarification of the situation at the Institute.

The campaign was intensified when the Anglo-Saxon Club of Hampton called a mass meeting at the courthouse on November 27, 1925, to be addressed by two noted racists: Maj. Ernest Sevier Cox, "ethnologist and explorer," and John Powell, "noted Virginia pianist." The leaders in the attack were drawn from the ranks of the local establishment and included Dr. J. Wilton Hope, president of the Hampton Post of the Anglo-Saxon Club, C. Vernon Spratley, judge of the Circuit Court, and Maj. E. Sclater Montague. Attorney Montague presided at this meeting of three hundred people and vigorously condemned Hampton's practices. He was particularly incensed by the fact that when the "almost nude" Denishawn Dancers performed at Ogden Hall, "the races were seated without reference to color." He made it clear that he himself never went anywhere near Hampton Institute and that he "stood for white supremacy and the complete separation of the races." Gregg was severely criticised for failing to attend this meeting. Apparently he made a decision not to defend publicly the social practices at Hampton and refused even to appear before legislative committees when they later held hearings on the segregation bill. But a faculty member of Hampton Institute, Maj. J. B. L. Buck, courageously defended the school at the courthouse meeting and urged the audience not to take any action against the college. Frank Foster, a Hampton teacher, greatly antagonized the audience by referring to them as "mongrels." He was told "politely" to leave and left his speech unfinished. Major Buck said he could not speak for the school but admitted that they did not segregate the audiences at Ogden Hall by race and that on occasion white and colored teachers not only sat together but actually ate together on campus. Evidently these atrocities motivated 300 citizens of Hampton to sign a resolve asking Delegate George A. Massenburg of Elizabeth City County to introduce a bill at the upcoming session of the legislature to segregate people by race at all public meetings. The resolution also protested "against the doctrines and teachings of social equality with its resultant tendency toward racial amalgamation and the indiscriminate seating of whites and blacks at public assemblages as fostered, fashioned and founded at Hampton Normal and Agricultural Institute."[77]

W. S. Copeland, editor of both the morning and evening Newport News papers, spoke at the mass meeting and kept the racist agitation alive thereafter by writing frequent editorials in his papers. He vigorously supported the Massenburg Bill, which was moving through the General Assembly early in 1926, while still assuring his readers that "it was not inspired by an unfriendliness toward the colored people" but was only to prevent any possible clash between the races on railroad and street cars.[78]

Taft's first response to the mass meeting held at the courthouse on November 27 was one of genuine indignation and disgust. He wrote Gregg: "This is calculated to make a man, unless he is a Minister, use profanity. I don't know what the Legislature of Virginia could do, though the ingenuity of fools is sometimes very great." The principal also contemptuously dismissed the Anglo-Saxon Club as a "little knot of fanatics who make up in noise what they lack in numbers. The meeting the other evening was engineered, I judge, with the hope of having me present to answer embarrassing questions." Having speedily recovered from his initial outburst of indignation, Taft retreated to his normal conservative stance and seconded Gregg's sentiments: "I . . . agree with you that the thing to do is to sit tight and let these cranks yell." A little later the chief justice praised an editorial in the Norfolk *Ledger-Dispatch,* which advocated leaving Hampton Institute alone, as being "useful following the fool declaration of those extremists who passed resolutions at Hampton."[79]

Believing that the best strategy was to keep a low profile during the controversy, Gregg did meet with about "half a dozen representative citizens of the town of Hampton the other evening at my house," but as usual he was too sanguine about the possible role which the "better Southerners" could play in abating racism at full cry. Delegate Massenburg of Hampton invited

Gregg to testify at the House of Delegates' General Laws Committee hearing on the bill, but the principal declined. The defense of the Institute was left to the presidents of Randolph-Macon College and of the University of Richmond, St. George Tucker, prominent Episcopalian clergyman of Richmond, and the president of the Richmond Chamber of Commerce, all of whom spoke against the bill as unnecessarily stirring up racial feelings. The Norfolk *Virginian Pilot* also objected to it editorially as did the two local white trustees of Hampton, Frank W. Darling and Homer L. Ferguson.[80]

But as might be expected in the racist atmosphere of the twenties, the Massenburg Bill passed the House of Delegates on February 5 by a vote of 64 to 2. It provided that the audience in every public hall must be segregated by race subject to fines of $100 to $500 for each offense; fines of $10–$25 could be levied against anyone who refused to be seated in his race's section of the hall. On the unlikely probability that the Senate might not pass the bill, the Newport News Anglo-Saxon Club held a meeting in the Chamber of Commerce on February 18 at which John Powell and Major Cox, author of *White America,* were the leading speakers. Powell made an hysterical appeal to the group to act, for if they didn't "your grandchildren will be negroids, the way things are shaping up in the state and country now."[81]

On January 20, a special meeting of Hampton's trustees on campus considered for the first time what was to be done about the "curious and disheartening agitation against the Institute." During the course of the meeting, Gregg said that perhaps his administration had not done the right thing in response to the movement and he offered to resign if that would help the situation. The Board discussed the matter while Gregg and his staff withdrew from the meeting temporarily. It was finally resolved that a committee of five be appointed by the chairman, to include the president of the Board, Chief Justice Taft, if he would consent to serve, to draw up a "dignified protest against the bill for the separation of white and colored people in public halls" to be transmitted to the General Assembly and also to be published.[82] Two trustees — Frank Darling, prominent Hampton sea food plant owner, and Homer Ferguson, president of the Newport News Shipbuilding and Drydock Company—did go to the House of Delegates hearing on the bill where they pleaded for a delay of two years so that "the situation would be corrected and separate seats would be provided for the audience in Ogden Hall" or they would resign from the Board. Evidently this position did not represent majority thinking of the trustees and in any case neither man did actually leave Hampton's Board.

The adjourned meeting of the Board was resumed on March 3 at the residence of the chief justice in Washington. Nine members were present (but not the only Black member, Dr. Moton, president of Tuskegee Institute). As the bill had already passed the House, they had the intention of asking Taft to write a letter requesting Governor Harry F. Byrd to veto the bill. But the chief justice expressed his opinion that in the circumstances an official protest "would be unwise, though such action might be desired by our colored constituency: the question is one to be settled by 'wise restraint' rather than by public protest." He even cautioned that a protest should be made to the governor after the bill's passage by the Senate only if the governor desired it. But in any event, he did not write any letter because, as he explained to his daughter, he resented the pressure by his colleagues to use his influential name and office on behalf of the institution.[83]

At least Taft seemingly recognized that many Black people wanted the school to take a forceful stand against this encroaching racism. Some of Hampton's Black faculty members had met with the Board of Trustees at its January 30 meeting,[84] and when the bill was passed by the Senate on March 9 by a vote of 30 to 5 and became law without the governor's signature on March 22, the Alumni Visitation Committee requested that the school test the constitutionality of the Massenburg Law. But the Institute's policy continued to be one of public passivity, although this was not done without a great deal of soul-searching, letterwriting, and meetings among concerned officials. Gregg himself had finally met with Governor Byrd on March 25. Several versions of a statement about future school policy if the law were passed had been written and revised, with the intention of presenting it to the governor.[85] But almost at the last minute Dr. James H. Dillard, an influential member of the General Education Board, persuaded Gregg that it would be inexpedient to give the governor any such written policy statement because "it would be regarded and misrepresented by the opposition as a token of our surrender and that it would be open to misconstruction also by the radical Negroes in a similar fashion."[86]

Among the trustees and other persons with close ties to Hampton, two points of view seem to have emerged as to the school's proper response to the new segregation law. Moton of Tuskegee put the case most strongly for challenging the constitutionality of the law in the courts, arguing that if the Institute acquiesced in it, many colored people would feel betrayed. On the other hand, most of Hampton's white friends seemed to have agreed with President Blackwell of Randolph-Macon College, who cautioned against challenging the law in court because "if by any chance it was found that this particular law was unconstitutional, or in any way faulty, the next legislature would devise a law that was not faulty. To take the matter to court would stir up all the feelings against Hampton that showed itself at the legislative hearings. Besides, it would be taken as proof that Hampton was using non-segregation in Ogden Hall as an entering wedge to break down all race distinction."[87]

Taft along with other influential men urged Gregg to a course of moderation and to follow the advice of legal counsel.[88] Fortunately the trustees recognized as was forcefully pointed out in Moton's letter and in the annual report of the Alumni Visitation Committee that "it would not be possible to impose upon our audiences the hard and fast segregation the law calls for," and they readily agreed with the opinion of John Weymouth, Hampton's lawyer, who recommended the school simply sidestep the law, which required segregation in "any place of public entertainment or public assemblage," by restricting attendance at all its paying functions to "persons connected with Hampton Institute and their specially invited guests."[89]

Gregg justified this course in a letter he penned to Taft "on the train" April 7, 1926:

I am not in the least eager, myself, to take the race separation law into the courts. The idea of putting the Institute into the position of fighting with the Commonwealth of Virginia is repellant. Such a course would again focus all the reactionary prejudices and smouldering enmities on Hampton Institute; and whatever we might win legally, we should lose what we most need to have and keep—the confidence and affection of the really representative people of Virginia,—which we still have, even after this past year's campaign of calumny. On the other hand, a quiet withdrawal of our privileges from public use will be comprehensible, dignified and appropriate.[90]

Taft replied immediately, endorsing this course of action: "I am delighted, too with the disposition that has been made in regard to the new legislation," and he also found Peabody's presentation of the new policy at the Anniversary Exercises on April 23 "admirable." To mitigate the effects of the Massenburg Law, Peabody stated that the college would consider "all Church and chapel exercises, all pay entertainments and all other assemblages" as private and so all students, alumni, employees and their families would be admitted as part of the school family, but no others would be allowed to attend except by invitation and no tickets would be on sale at the door of public meetings. An extensive list of persons wishing to attend Institute functions regularly was compiled and used in deciding which outsiders might be admitted.[91]

Gregg's policy of avoiding a legal confrontation was not popular with segments of the Hampton community who evidently doubted the sincerity of his commitment to Black rights. His personal views were expressed in answer to a letter from Ralph Earl of Denver University on March 23, 1926, in which the principal strongly condemned race prejudice—calling it incompatible with democracy and with Christianity.[92] But the whole controversy certainly did little to dispel the aura of conservatism at Hampton Institute and seemed to strengthen the ultra-conservatism into which Taft increasingly wrapped himself as he grew older.

In October 1927 a student protest movement broke out at Hampton in reaction against what the students felt were arbitrary and overly restrictive rules and poor instruction in certain areas. The immediate cause of the ensuing student strike was the showing of a documentary film in Ogden Hall on the evening of Saturday, October 8 during which the lights were purposely kept on by order of the administration. The movement took the form of noncooperation with such college rituals as singing grace at Sunday evening dinner and spirituals (then called plantation songs) at the vesper service. A student protest committee was organized which presented its concerns to the administration in the form of a petition. Many of these requests concerned upgrading the academic program, recognition of the student council, liberalization of the extremely puritanical rules of student conduct, and recruiting faculty members who were more sympathetic to the Black point of view. The students further supported the protest movement by refusing to go to classes on Monday, October 10. President Gregg refused to negotiate with the student protest committee until they abandoned the strike, and on Tuesday the students did go back to work. But then the principal, disregarding the advise of staff members who urged leniency, threatened retaliation against any student strike leaders, and the movement resumed again the next day. On Thursday morning, October 13, Gregg closed the school and summarily dismissed most of the members of the protest committee (with the notable exception of a student informer). When classes resumed October 25, more than 200 students were gone because they had participated in the strike or refused to sign the pledge of loyalty as a means of being reenrolled. These dismissals and suspensions eliminated virtually the entire leadership of the most prominent student organizations.[93]

The administration put forth its case in a form letter which was sent to parents or guardians of the students as early as Friday, October 14, when it had closed the school and expelled the student leaders, who were blamed for "insubordination or of inciting others to insubordination." Gregg telegraphed Taft, as president of the Board of Trustees, on Saturday, October 15, to assure him that most students were desirous of remaining or returning to the school, and that there had been "no violence and no destruction of school property."[94] Taft was totally out of sympathy with the student protestors. "Considering the advantages that they enjoy over and above their fellows in the matter of a free education, it is difficult to be patient with such an exhibition, and they ought to be taught a lesson that we shall not be bothered again. It is a disposition to ape the absurdities of other institutions—public schools—in some cities where the children are influenced by the wild ideas of their parents in the matter of democratic control of the school by the children." And, continuing, the chief justice fully supported Gregg's hard line:

I am delighted that you have taken such positive steps. I am glad that you have dismissed four or five ringleaders, and I hope that you will let any of the others go who upon examination prove to be of the same class. It really is difficult to be patient with such silly dealings. I mean silly only in the sense that they have no justification and are childish, but not silly in the injury that they would do to the institution as a whole, showing that they are not worthy of receiving the great benefit that the institution confers.[95]

Gregg was greatly encouraged by Taft's support and in writing him on the nineteenth assured him that "the repentant sinners are returning in increasing numbers, and we expect to be operating on regular schedules by next Tuesday" and that the "alumni and parents have stood by us solidly, if we may judge from all the letters, telegrams and other reports of their senti-ments that have come to us." Taft was apparently fully con-vinced that the fifty-two students who were actually dismissed had no real grievances or support from anyone. Gregg seem-ingly was still pretty concerned about the way he had handled the strike as he was eager to report to Taft even in late November that "school affairs seem to be going on smoothly. We have 862 students at present, nearly the same number as last year at this time, if I remember rightly. Dr. Phenix has just returned from a trip through Kentucky, in which he visited a large number of Negro schools. He reports everywhere em-phatic approval of our course in handling the strike. The critical articles in the last number of the *Crisis* will not damage us seriously, I imagine."[96]

After the student strike, Taft was kept informed as usual of developments at Hampton, but because his health was failing he was not intimately involved in its affairs. Although he finally resigned from the Supreme Court on February 3, 1930, he was still president of Hampton's Board of Trustees at the time of his death on March 8, 1930.

Taft knew what had happened to the rights of Black people since Reconstruction. At the time he was active in Hampton's affairs, the mass of Black people had been effectively disfranchised and were subject to every type of discrimination and injustice. But he was not inclined to antagonize the white southerners by demanding that they accord Black people at least their legal rights. Instead he relied on the belief that the "better Southerners" were potentially the best friends the Black people had and that once they had become stable wage earners, through Hampton's type of training, these good Southerners would see that they were treated fairly. Most of the trustees and administrators of Hampton with whom Taft came in contact shared this outlook on the American race problem, and seemingly many of the Black people connected with education also adopted this outlook. Only an occasional dissident voice, such as W. E. B. Du Bois's in the *Crisis,* reached Taft, and he was not persuaded by such people because he considered them radical and irresponsible leaders.

Taft's principal contribution to Hampton was undoubtedly the prestige which being president of the United States and chief justice of the United States lent to his position as president of Hampton's Board of Trustees, especially in fund-raising activities. Taft's intimate connection with, and great interest in, Hampton's whole program were partially responsible for several of the larger bequests which the school received from major philanthropists. His connection with national politicians most probably helped the school hold onto its land in the face of several federal encroachments and in turn he may have helped various Black people, recommended by Hampton's principal, to get the government jobs they wanted. Taft's connection with Hampton Institute marked the high point in the school's involvement with the most important national political leaders. Almost every president from the time of Hampton's founding to Taft's administration visited the college, but none did so after Taft left office. One can only contemplate the course of Taft's connection with Hampton with a feeling of satisfaction that at a critical period in its development the school should have had even the part-time assistance of a president and a chief justice.

Notes

1. William H. Taft, Address of William Howard Taft, secretary of war, on behalf of Hampton Institute, Virginia, at Plymouth Church, Brooklyn, N.Y., Mar. 16, 1908, p. 14, and "The South and the National Government," address delivered at the dinner of the North Carolina Society of New York at the Hotel Astor, Dec. 7, 1908, p. 11, in Taft Papers, Archives, Hampton Institute, Hampton, Va.

2. William H. Taft, "Southern Industrial Education and the Negro," address delivered in Carnegie Hall under the auspices of the Armstrong Association, Feb. 23, 1909, *Southern Workman* 38 (1909), 591.

3. Remarks by Taft at Hampton Institute, June 8, 1912, p. 2, Taft Papers.

4. William Howard Taft, "Hampton's Gift to the Nation," *Southern Workman* 48 (1919), 301.

5. Remarks by Taft at Hampton Institute, June 8, 1912, pp. 2–3, Taft Papers.

6. "Mr. Taft's Address," Apr. 27, 1917, *Southern Workman* 46 (1917), 361.

7. "Hampton's Gift to the Nation," p. 302.

8. Donald L. Anderson, *William Howard Taft: A Conservative's Conception of the Presidency* (Ithaca, N.Y.: Cornell University Press, 1973), p. 193.

9. "The South and the National Government," p. 10, Taft Papers; "The Negro Problem in America," *Southern Workman* 50 (1921), 10.

10. "The South and the National Government" pp. 11, 13, Taft Papers; Alpheus Thomas Mason, *William Howard Taft, Chief Justice* (New York: Simon and Schuster, 1964), pp. 14–15.

11. "The South and the National Government," pp. 11–12, Taft Papers.

12. William H. Taft, "The Negro Problem in America," *Southern Workman* 50 (1921), p. 12.

13. Taft, "Southern Industrial Education," p. 591.

14. The resolution read: "That this Board desires to represent to the President of the United States the profound sense of humiliation and shame with which their constituency, both black and white, and at both the South as well as at the North, observes the continued practice of lynching with its revolting horrors and the resulting degradation of its perpetrators. We venture to urge that the President, having expressed in a letter of 1918 his deep concern for this national disgrace, continue to use his great influence to check the calamity, assuring him that such action will be welcomed by great numbers of citizens who are now seriously disquieted and alarmed" (Minutes of the Board of Trustees, May 1, 1919, 3:387, Archives, Hampton Institute).

15. "The Negro Problem in America," p. 14.

16. "The South and the National Government," p. 14, Taft Papers.

17. Address on behalf of Hampton Institute, p. 16, Taft Papers; "The Negro Problem in America," p. 15.

18. Mason, *Taft*, p. 14.

19. William Howard Taft, "The Spirit of Hampton," *Southern Workman* 43 (1914), 409.

20. "The Negro Problem in America," p. 15.

21. Address on behalf of Hampton Institute, pp. 2, 15–16, Taft Papers.

22. "Hampton Notes," *Southern Workman* 44 (1915), 361–62.

23. Taft, "Southern Industrial Education," p. 588.

24. "The South and the National Government," p. 14, Taft Papers.

25. Ibid., p. 16.

26. "The Negro Problem in America," p. 14.

27. Ibid., p. 12.

28. "The Spirit of Hampton," p. 410.

29. "Anniversary Echoes: II, William Howard Taft," *Southern Workman* 50 (1921), 415.

30. Address on behalf of Hampton Institute, p. 9, Taft Papers.

31. Ibid., p. 12; William A. Aery, "Taft Day at Hampton," *Southern Workman* 38 (1909), 655.

32. "Anniversary Echoes: II," p. 416.

33. "Anniversary Echoes: I, Nannie Burroughs," *Southern Workman* 50 (1921), 413–14.

34. "Anniversary Echoes: II," pp. 415–16.

35. William H. Taft, "Hampton's Relation to Race Problems," *Southern Workman* 38 (1909), 649–50, and Aery, "Taft Day at Hampton," ibid., pp. 650–55. President Taft even echoed Garfield's criticisms of 1867 when he said of American education, "We had been struggling along for several hundred years with our system of education."

36. "President Taft Visits Hampton," *Hampton Student,* June 15, 1912, p. 2; "Summer Happenings," *Southern Workman* 41 (1912), 583.

37. President Taft's speech at Hampton Institute, June 8, 1912, p. 1, Taft Papers.

38. Taft to Hollis Burke Frissell, June 4, 1912, in Hollis B. Frissell Papers, Archives, Hampton Institute. All subsequent letters cited are in the Frissell Papers unless otherwise noted; *Hampton Student,* June 15, 1912, p. 2.

39. Frissell to Taft, Jan. 31, 1912, and Jan. 7, 1913.

40. Taft to Frissell, Aug. 21 and Dec. 25, 1909, in answer to Frissell's letter of Dec. 24, 1909.

41. Frissell to Taft, Nov. 29, 1912; Taft to Frissell, Nov. 30, 1912.

42. Frissell to Taft, Dec. 28, 1910; Taft [signed by Secretary of the Interior Norton] to Frissell, Dec. 29, 1910.

43. Frissell to Taft, Feb. 1906.

44. Frissell to Taft, Apr. 24 and Nov. 10, 1911.

45. Frissell to Taft, May 27, 1912; Taft to Frissell, May 29, 1912.

46. Frissell to Taft, Nov. 29, 1912; Taft to Frissell, Nov. 30, 1912.

47. Taft [signed by Taft's secretary, Mitscher] to Frissell, Dec. 18, 1912; Frissell to Taft, Dec. 19, 1912.

48. Frederick C. Hicks, *William Howard Taft: Yale Professor of Law and New Haven Citizen* (New Haven: Yale University Press, 1945), p. 13; Taft to Frissell, May 11, 1914, and April 27, 1915.

49. Frissell to Taft, Dec. 2 and 8, 1913; Mar. 8 and July 28, 1915; Taft to Frissell, July 22, 1916.

50. Frissell to Taft, Jan. 4, 1915, and June 12, 1917; Taft to Frissell, Jan. 11, 1915.

51. Frissell to Taft, Feb. 16, 1915; Taft to Frissell, Feb. 17, 1915.

52. Frissell to Taft, Jan. 2, 1915; Taft to Frissell, Jan. 11, 1915.

53. Minutes of Board of Trustees Meeting, Apr. 22, 1915, 3:183; Taft to Frissell, Apr. 27, 1915.

54. J. B. Aleshire, quartermaster general, to Taft, July 9, 1915.

55. Frissell to Taft, Dec. 11, 1916; Minutes of Executive Committee of the Board of Trustees, Mar. 14, 1918, 3:328–29. The government wanted to purchase all of Shellbanks Farm in November 1917 but evidently did not follow through when the college wanted $300 an acre (ibid., Nov. 8, 1917, 3:300).

56. Minutes of Board of Trustees Meeting, Oct. 9, 1918, 3:353; Minutes of Executive Committee of the Board of Trustees, Dec. 5, 1918, 3:330.

57. Minutes of Special Meeting of the Board, Feb. 2, 1920, 3:407; ibid., Jan. 31, 1921, 3:472, 473.

58. Minutes of Board of Trustees, Apr. 29, 1920, 3:419; Minutes of Special Meeting of the Board, June 17, 1921, 3:473; ibid., Jan. 30, 1922, 3:485.

59. James E. Gregg to Taft, Apr. 28, 1924, Taft Papers, ser. 3, Manuscript Division, Library of Congress.

60. Gregg to Taft, Feb. 2 and 28, 1921, ibid.

61. William H. Taft, "The Negro in Politics," Philadelphia *Public Ledger,* Jan. 8, 1921, Gregg Administration Clipping File, no. 7, Archives, Hampton Institute.

62. "A Reply to Mr. Taft on 'The Negro in Politics,' " the Inter-Racial Committee of Philadelphia, ibid.

63. Taft to Gregg, Feb. 7, 1921, and Gregg to Taft, Apr. 7, 1921, Taft Papers, ser. 3, LC.

64. Gregg to Taft, Feb. 10 and Apr. 7, 1921, ibid.

65. Gregg to Taft, Apr. 21, 1921, and Taft to Gregg, Apr. 27, 1921, ibid.

66. Gregg to Taft, Mar. 1 and 6, 1928, and Taft to Gregg, Mar. 8, 1928, ibid.

67. Taft to Lloyd George, Oct. 11, 1923, ibid.

68. Taft to Gregg, Apr. 30, 1924, ibid.

69. Gregg to Taft, Feb. 3, 16, 20, 25, 1925, Taft to Gregg, Feb. 5, May 22, 1925, Taft to Horace A. Moses, Feb. 11, 1925, Taft to Harris Dickson, May 22, 1925, Clarence H. Kelsey to Taft, Mar. 30, 1925, ibid.

70. John D. Rockefeller, Jr., to Gregg, Feb. 13, 1925, Massenburg Law File, Archives, Hampton Institute.

71. Gregg to Taft, Jan. 24, Mar. 25, Apr. 8, 1925, and Taft to Gregg, Jan. 26 and Mar. 26, 1925, Taft Papers, ser. 3, LC.

72. Richard I. Manning to Gregg, Aug. 12, 1925, Massenburg Law File.

73. Taft to Gregg, Aug. 23, 1925, Taft Papers, ser. 3, LC.

74. Gregg to Taft, Sept. 3, 1925, ibid.

75. Newport News *Daily Press,* Mar. 15, 1925, p. 4.

76. Copy of letter sent by Anglo-Saxon Clubs of America, Archives, Hampton Institute; Newport News *Daily Press,* July 17, 1925, p. 4.

77. Newport News *Daily Press,* Nov. 28, 1925, pp. 1–2.

78. Ibid., Jan. 28, 1926, p. 4.

79. Taft to Gregg, Nov. 30, Dec. 5, 1925, Jan. 8, 1926, and Gregg to Taft, Dec. 1, 1925, Taft Papers, ser. 3, LC.

80. Gregg to Taft, Dec. 30, 1925, ibid.; Norfolk *Virginian Pilot,* Feb. 2, 1926, Massenburg Law File.

81. Newport News *Daily Press,* Feb. 19, 1926, p. 1.

82. Minutes of Board of Trustees, 4:165.

83. Ibid., 4:175; Mason, *Taft,* p. 275, quoting letter to Taft to Helen Taft Manning.

84. Newport News *Star,* Feb. 4, 1926, clipping in Massenburg Law File. This meeting was not reported in the Board minutes, however.

85. Gregg to Taft, Mar. 10, 24, 26, Apr. 3 and 7, 1926; Taft to George F. Peabody, Mar. 16, 1926; Taft to Gregg Mar. 26 and Apr. 5, 1926; and Jackson Davis to Gregg, Apr. 13, 1926, Taft Papers, ser. 3, LC. Governor Byrd told Gregg, at their meeting on March 25, that he had allowed the race separation bill to become law without his signature the previous day, but he made it plain that he considered the bill extremely regrettable and said that he did not approve of it, that if a member of the General Assembly he would have voted against it, but that in view of all the circumstances—especially the facts that it was passed in both House and Senate by overwhelming majorities and that when it came to him the General Assembly had adjourned, so that he could not, in vetoing the bill, return it for fresh consideration by the members—he did not feel warranted in preventing it becoming law.

86. Gregg to Taft, Mar. 24, 1926, ibid.

87. Robert R. Moton to Gregg, Mar. 25, 1926, and R. E. Blackwall to Gregg, Apr. 20, 1926, Massenburg Law File.

88. Taft to Gregg, Apr. 5, 1926, and Jackson Davis to Gregg, Apr. 13, 1926, Massenburg Law File.

89. Report of Hampton Alumni Visitation Committee to Board of Trustees, Apr. 19, 1926, p. 1, Taft Papers, ser. 3, LC; Gregg to John Weymouth, Mar. 31, 1926, Weymouth to Gregg, Apr. 22, 1926, Massenburg Law File; Minutes of Board of Trustees, Apr. 22, 1926, 4:195–96.

90. Gregg to Taft, Apr. 7, 1926, Taft Papers, ser. 3, LC.

91. Taft to Gregg, Apr. 28, 1926, ibid.; Minutes of Board of Trustees, Apr.

22, 1926, 4:195– 96. The list is in the file labeled "Race Separation," Archives, Hampton Institute.

92. Gregg to Ralph Earl, Mar. 23, 1926, Race Separation File.

93. This account is taken largely from the manuscript article "The Hampton Institute Strike of 1926: A Case Study in Student Protest," by Edward K. Graham, Centennial Historian, Hampton Institute, 1968.

94. Gregg to Taft, Oct. 15, 1927, Taft Papers, ser. 3, LC.

95. Taft to Gregg, Oct. 17, 1927, ibid.

96. Gregg to Taft, Oct. 19 and Nov. 28, 1927, and Taft to Gregg, Oct. 27, 1927, ibid.

To Make a Scholar Black:
A Tribute to Jay Saunders Redding
Frances A. Grimes

THE CAREER OF Jay Saunders Redding as a recognized scholar spans a period of more than forty years. During this period he has distinguished himself as a teacher at Morehouse College, Louisville Municipal College, Southern University, Elizabeth City State College, Hampton Institute, George Washington University, and Cornell University. In addition, he has been the recipient of coveted fellowships, such as the Rockefeller and the Guggenheim, and of numerous awards and citations for scholarly and humanitarian achievements. He has written eight books and edited several others, authored numerous articles, essays, and book reviews, lectured in foreign countries as well as across the United States, and served as director of the Division of Research and Publication of the National Endowment for the Humanities. Having recently retired from his position as Ernest I. White Professor of American Studies and Humane Letters at Cornell University, he continues there, as professor emeritus, many of the scholarly pursuits for which he has long been known and respected.

Such a list of accomplishments as Saunders Redding can boast is no mean achievement for a Black man born in this country in 1906. For as one thinks in general about the social forces that conspired against minority groups in the early part of this century and as one focuses in particular on Redding's background, he becomes mindful of the mental torture, anguish, and deliberation out of which the distinguished scholar necessarily forged his career.

At the beginning of his partially autobiographical *No Day of Triumph*, Redding speaks of the tension he felt as a youngster growing up in Wilmington, Delaware, in a family where two points of view on race and religion were represented by his two grandmothers. As he details one of the visits of his father's

Jay Saunders Redding

mother, Grandma Redding, he pauses to give a description of
her:

I do not know how she managed to give the impression of shining
with a kind of deadly hard glare, for she was always clothed entirely in
black and her black, even features were as hard and lightless as stone.
I never saw a change of expression on her features. She never smiled.

In anger her face turned slowly, dully gray, but her thin nostrils never flared, her long mouth never tightened. She was tall and fibrous and one of her ankles had been broken when she was a girl and never properly set, so that she walked with a defiant limp.[1]

Grandma Redding's ankle had been broken when her master, Caleb Wrightson, had flung a chunk of wood at her when, at ten, she had been captured trying to escape from slavery along with a young woman of eighteen. She never forgot her master and all he symbolized. Indeed, after relating to her grandchildren the story of the attempted escape and its aftermath, she concluded, "An' ol' man Caleb stank lik' a pes'-house from the rottin' of his stomick 'fore he died an' went t' hell, an' his boys died in the wo' an' went to hell."[2]

Redding's maternal grandmother, Grandma Conway, was the exact opposite:

Grandma Conway said "Good Morning" as if she were pronouncing the will of God. A woman as squat and solid as a tree stump, she had a queer knurl of religious thought and character that no ax of eclecticism could cleave. She had great bouts of religious argument with whoever would argue with her. Even though her adversary sat but two feet away, she would shout out her disputes and half rise threateningly, her gray serge breast lifting and falling as if she had been running uphill. She often frightened our young friends in this manner, awed them into speechlessness; and when she had done this, her green-yellow eyes would blink very fast and her fat, yellow little fists would fly to her chest and beat gently there in laughter.[3]

It was on a hot Sunday morning in August during Redding's childhood that Grandma Conway, who had been visiting the Reddings for a month, and Grandma Redding, who was making one of her usual unannounced visits from her home fifty miles away, finally met. The wide divergence between the two which Redding had sensed even as a young boy was brought to the fore. Offering the prayers at the breakfast table as was her custom when visiting her daughter's household, Grandma Conway closed her prayers by including the "intruder" among those for whom she asked special blessings: "And Redding's ma, Lord. She's with us this morning. She has her affliction, Holy One, and we can hardly notice it, but it's an affliction on

her. Bless her. Teach her that affliction chasteneth a righteous
heart and only the wicked are bowed down. Bless her, dear
God, and bless us all."[4]

On this note, Grandma Redding, who had declined as being
"no comp'ny prayin' one" when Grandma Conway had earlier
offered to allow her to lead the prayers, took up the supplica-
tion. Referring to the thousand years that had passed since
Jesus was on earth, she spoke of the "mean business" that had
come into being since that absence—"slav'ry," "devilment and
hate an' wo' an' some being one thing and some another."
Then, summoning what would seem to her the most meaningful blessings for the younger generation as well as for her own
and at the same time obliquely referring to her own affliction,
she closed her prayers taciturnly: "Now, bless these young 'uns.
Bless 'em on earth. It don't matter 'bout us ol' ones. We'se skit-
terin' down the rocky hill anyhow. Bless us in the everlastin'.
But these young 'uns, they's climbin' up. All I ast be You keep
'em from the knowin' an' the manbirthed sins o' blackness.
We'se bent on knees to Your will, Lord Jesus. Amen."[5]

According to Redding, Grandma Redding's prayer apparently had no lasting effect upon others who heard it, but,
young as he was, its impression upon him was profound:

In time to come it was to be as a light thrown upon Grandma Redding's character, and by reflection, upon Grandma Conway's. It was
only later, of course, that I had any intellectual comprehension of the
basis of the contrast between them. For many years I continued to
think of Grandma Redding as a strange, bitterly choleric old woman
and that her irascibility was somehow a part of her blackness. I could
not help this absurdity then, for ours was an upper-class Negro
family, the unwitting victim of our own culture complexes; deeply
sensitive to the tradition of ridicule and inferiority attaching to color;
hating the tradition and yet inevitably absorbing it.[6]

Though Redding did not inherit the fair skin of his mother's
side of the family ("I was dark"), nonetheless, during his childhood he often escaped being the victim of "color-struck"
teachers because of the "upper-class" status his family enjoyed.
But to one sensitive to the demands of fair play, an obviously
accorded favor was more likely to bring distress than jubilation.
Redding remembers, for instance, his first oratorical contest, in

which he vied against his peer Tom Cephus. Fully aware that
Cephus, whose voice was vibrant and masculine, had the edge
in the contest, Redding had burst into tears from fright and
nervous exhaustion in the middle of his delivery. In his turn,
Cephus had faced the audience with superb control and poise.
Redding was certain that Cephus had won; and he was
stunned, as was the majority of the audience, when the judge,
in icy Bostonian accent, announced Cephus as the second-place
winner, him as the first. But deep down they all knew why the
results were as they were: Cephus was not only "a gangling
dark fellow," he was from the "lower class." Redding dropped
out of school for a week. Cephus dropped out of school for a
year. And, as Redding later recalls, "the boy who won and lost"
died before he reached the full bloom of manhood.[7]

But if the Negro world of Wilmington offered Redding favored situations, however unwelcome, uninvited, and uncom-
fortable, the white world with which he found himself sur-
rounded when he went to college at Brown University did not.
As Redding records in *On Being Negro in America,* his father had
advised him as he left for Brown, "Son, remember you're a
Negro. You'll have to do twice as much twice better than your
classmates. . . . Out East you may feel it less because there're
fewer Negroes, or for the same reason, you may feel it more.
Some say one thing, some the other. But no matter where you
go in this country, you'll never get away from being made to
know that you are a Negro."[8]

In 1925, when Redding entered Brown University, one was
"made to know that he was a Negro" through discrimination on
the one hand and through isolation on the other. A Negro's
white associates snubbed him or slighted him and occasionally
in class his instructors uttered racially insulting remarks or
committed overt acts of discrimination. A Negro's Black
associates (these were few in number; there were only three
other Negroes at Brown, at various times, during Redding's
undergraduate years) took precautions not to associate with
him anywhere on campus except in the privacy of his room,
and even this association took place under the cover of night
with shades drawn. Negroes wanted to avoid the appearance of
clannishness.[9]

The characteristic overt discrimination and the careful, self-imposed isolation took its toll on Negroes in colleges all over New England. Strained and drained of self-respect, Clyde Bastrop, the only other Negro student at Brown during Redding's second year there, threatened to leave the school:

There must be some place better than this. . . . I can find a place somewhere. This isn't the place for me. I feel like everybody's staring at me, all these white guys waiting for me to make a bad break. Things I'd do without thinking about them, I do now like they were the most important things in the whole damned world. . . . We're always talking about being casual. All right. But what do we do? . . . We put on the damnedest airs in the world. We're showing off. Casually, casually, by Christ! . . . I'm sick of being casual! I want to be honest and sincere about something. I want to stop feeling like I'll fall apart if I unclench my teeth. Oh Christ![10]

Bastrop did leave Brown as he had threatened. And Redding never saw him again, for shortly after he left, he took his own life in the bathroom of his parents' home in Cleveland.[11]

Such impressions and incidents as these that were a part of Redding's childhood and young adult years were not to leave him psychologically untouched. On the one hand, his own experiences and Grandma Redding cautioned him to beware of whites; on the other, Grandma Conway and the optimism she represented insisted that he could be a person in spite of his black skin, his Negroness. Perhaps the best example of the strain imposed on him by the tension between these extremes is seen through an experience he had while teaching at Louisville Municipal College. Standing and looking out the window of an empty classroom on a winter day, Redding saw a young white woman, clad only in a ragged slip, lurching and staggering in her back yard. Redding could not determine whether the young woman's convulsive movements were indicative of intoxication or illness. And though he pitied her as she floundered toward the outhouse in the snow, he at the same time felt "a gloating satisfaction that she was white." Having watched her struggle and finally lie still after pitching face downward in the snow, he called the police and reported, "There's a drunken woman lying the back yard on Eighth Street, seven-hundred block." Almost an hour later, from his place at the window,

Redding saw a policeman arrive on the scene. In the next morning's paper he read that the young woman had died following an epileptic seizure.[12]

The aftermath of this experience, by Redding's own admission, left smudges and scars on his psyche: "I offer no excuses for my part in this wretched episode. Excuses are unavailing. The experiences of my Negroness, in a section where such experiences have their utmost meaning in fear and degradation, canceled out humaneness. How many times have I heard Negroes mutter, when witness to some misfortune befallen a white person, 'What the hell! He's white, isn't he?' What the exact psychological mechanism of this is, I cannot say, but certainly the frustration of human sympathy and kindness is a symptom of a dangerous trauma."[13]

Redding had written *On Being Negro in America* as a means of seeking "a purge, a catharsis, wholeness." Early in the book he reasoned that by observing his own "fears, doubts, ambitions, hates" he would be able "to get rid of something that is unhealthy in me (that is perhaps unhealthy in most Americans) and so face the future with some tranquility."[14] But however purgative the writing of the volume, its effects were not to endure for a lifetime as he had hoped.

At the beginning of *An American in India,* an account of the three-month tour he made in India in 1952 for the State Department, Redding speaks of accepting the assignment to help interpret American life to the people of India as a means of testing his freedom from the emotional baggage he had jettisoned by writing *On Being Negro in America.* He had vowed to himself that during his excursion in India he would simply tell the truth and not be concerned about what the truth would do to America. "The national unit called America meant nothing to me now. At last my hopeful, loving hate for her had died, and the final result of the American experience had been to force me to depersonalize myself. I was glad. I was free."[15]

Before Redding had completed his trip, however, he found he could not maintain his depersonalized declaration of freedom. During a question-and-answer period after he had spoken before the Mysindia Writers and Artists Conference, he was bombarded with questions. From various spots in the room, one Indian after another rose from a sea of inscrutable faces to interrogate him suspiciously about the policy of the American government. Finally, one of the questioners read a statement to the effect that the capitalist system could survive only by promoting armed conflict and then asked whether that was the reason that the American government encouraged war in Korea. Redding countered that he would not accept the premise, insisted that all concerned be clear, first of all, on the phrase "capitalist system," and then proceeded to defend the competitive system of free enterprise in America. Voices sprang at him from all over the room, accusing him of evading the question and insisting that he answer it.[16] Anger boiling within him, Redding stood before his brown-skinned, taut-faced adversaries and felt the resolve with which he had boldly and aloofly begun his Indian excursion slipping from him:

I tried to examine my thoughts with cool curiosity. Why should I care what these people thought of America? Where was my "clinical" perspective, the substance of my private boast that I would simply tell the truth and let it go at that? Take it or leave it. Why should I be emotionally involved? But all at once I knew I could not help myself. I was involved because I was American and because I had to be in-volved in all that happened to America in the minds of people who were not Americans. I stood there feeling and thinking this.[17]

It must have been extremely difficult for Redding to summon this emotion. It must have been wrenched from him, as it were. For from almost the moment of his arrival in India he had been constantly reminded by the Indians of his kinship to them by skin color and of America's conscious and consistent sup-pression of its own Negro community and, in general, of the colored peoples of the world.[18]

Back in the United States after the trip to India, Redding held to the agonizing decision he had reached as he stood before the Mysindia Writers and Artists Conference. In great demand as a speaker, he delivered addresses and lectures not only in the environs of Hampton Institute, at which he continued to teach for fourteen years after his return, but all across the nation. Whenever the subject on which he spoke in any way concerned the position of Blacks in this country, he never failed to give his audience the message of hope and reasoned optimism at which he himself had arrived so painfully.

In 1956, for instance, in a speech delivered before the Contemporary Club, after reviewing incidents designed to perpetuate segregation which were taking place across the United States, and especially in Virginia, Redding pled the cause of the integrationist: "The way of the segregationist has failed, and the highest constitutional authority has declared it a failure. What the integrationist wants is a trial of his way—a trial begun with determination, carried on with patience, and conducted with foresight." Similarly, after acknowledging the obstacles with which Blacks in America had been historically and systematically faced, he challenged the graduating class of 1959 at Crispus Attucks High School in Indianapolis to press forward in the struggle for the realization of a dream: "We are today too close to fulfilling the dream of human equality. . . not to intensify our striving for it. Please understand the implications of that statement. Dreams do not happen by themselves. . . . The Emancipation Proclamation was not signed because of the operation of blind impulse. The Thirteenth, Fourteenth, and Fifteenth amendments were not added to the Constitution because of historical imperative. These things came about because certain men, exerting on events the pressure of learning and liberal thought, of love and brotherhood, chose to bring them about." And, in Philadelphia in 1963, in an address on modern African literature before the national meeting of Alpha Phi Alpha Fraternity, he predicted the eventual coming of age of African writers by comparing them to American Negro writers. The Negro writer, he implied, now stood "free on a mountain top," felt free to write what he liked because the time was rapidly approaching when he no longer needed to be concerned about the clash of Negro and non-Negro cultures in the United States.[19]

The message of his speeches, that Blacks should not admit disillusionment or thoughts of separation from the American fabric, then, reflected the attitude that Redding had held before the excursion to India, before his depersonalized declaration of freedom. It agreed with the point of view he had expressed to the editorial board at Lippincott, the publishers for whom he had written *They Came in Chains,* "the Negro book" in the Peoples of America Series. The editors had suggested that considerable space be spent on the Negro's African background. But Redding had maintained that while he believed it would be necessary to refer to that background from time to time, he did not see it as a chapter in the story. He saw the story he was to tell as predominantly one of acculturation, as America, he argued, was home for the second generation of Negro slaves. Thus, in telling the Negro story, he would also be telling the American story.[20] Redding was to present this point of view again in *The Lonesome Road,* in which he wove "the story of the Negro's part in America" through accounts of the lives of ascendant Negro leaders in the various periods of American history.[21]

One may adopt the opinion that such statements and points of view as Redding made and held in the fifties and in the first half of the sixties could be indicative of the wave and the temper then sweeping the country so far as Blacks were concerned. In 1954 the Supreme Court had reached its momentous school desegregation decision, and in the late fifties and early sixties sit-in demonstrations and freedom rides by sympathetic whites as well as Blacks were the order of the day. Many Blacks held the optimism and ultimate faith in the integration and acculturation to which Redding habitually referred. In the late sixties and the early seventies, however, Blacks became disillusioned by their failure to realize the immediate ideals that the fifties and sixties had both promised and suggested could be attained, and they took a longer and more critical look at history and began to rally to cries and slogans of Black pride and Black awareness. But Redding, who had arrived at his position through agonizing intellection, remained firm. Asked in 1971 during an interview with the *Washington Post* whether he still believed in the ideal of integration at a time when the apparent national temper of Blacks had become one favoring limited separation and building independent institutions, he replied:

Yes, I still believe in it. Once Blacks in America have consolidated power in various fields and have been able to use that power in viable ways, they're still going to be living in a society that ideally is multiracial, multicultural. . . .

Of course I want to maintain my identity as a black man. But I also want my identity not to interfere with any desire I might have to associate with, to do business with, to work with people who are non-black. Let me keep my identity, but don't make my blackness a penalty. I don't see how we can survive as a people unless we integrate.[22]

Redding's proclaimed belief in integration during the years when the separatist point of view was more popular was to be transmitted into action on the scholarly front. During the same interview, he spoke of integrating subject matter in the classroom:

I'm going to teach a course next semester in American literature, and in this course I'm going to try to integrate into the corpus of American literary expression the works of blacks. When I talk, for instance, about Hoosier poets like James Whitcomb Riley, I'm also going to talk about the black dialect poets who are of the same school. Their subject matter was different, but it's the same school.

And when I talk about the novel of social protest, I'm going to talk about Richard Wright. These are American works, after all. They ought to be integrated.

Now retired from the classroom, but not from the scholarly activity which has characterized so much of his life, Redding continues to be an integrationist. There can be no better indication of this than his response to a question posed him during the summer of 1975. Asked whether he thought Blacks should participate in the nation's observance of the Bicentennial, he replied unhesitantly, "Certainly, for Blacks have contributed greatly to the history of this nation." Redding then reported that he had been asked by the National Association for State and Local History to write the Bicentennial history of his native state, Delaware, and that, though he had not decided whether he would undertake the project, his hesitancy in no way reflected negative feelings about the matter because of his race. "I have other things on my mind, and I am afraid that doing the history will interfere disastrously."[23]

During the 1920s Countee Cullen, one of the luminaries of the Harlem Renaissance, penned the poem "Yet Do I Marvel."

In it he acknowledged his belief that God could explain all sorts of seemingly inscrutable phenomena—from why "the little buried mole continues blind" to whether "merely brute caprice dooms Sisyphus / To struggle up a never-ending stair." This being true, however, Cullen suggests that God would still be hard put to explain one phenomenon. "Yet do I marvel," he says in the closing lines of the poem, "at this curious thing: / To make a poet black, and bid him sing! "[24]

In 1939 the phrase "to make a poet black" appeared as the title of Redding's first book, a poignant analysis of Black American poetry. In the preface Redding implied that he would do in his volume what Cullen, to emphasize the difficulty of a situation, had suggested would pose a problem for man's superior: he could explain what had bade Black poets sing, having theorized that "almost from the beginning the literature of the Negro had been literature either of purpose or necessity."[25]

Redding was to address this subject again in 1958 when he delivered a paper, "The Negro Writer and His Relationship to His Roots," at the first conference of Negro writers held in the United States. His point was the same as it had been in his book, only this time he used metaphor to make it. Likening the Negro writer to a hunter, he remarked, "On the one hand, the jungle; on the other, the resourceful hunter to clear it. The jungle, where lurks the beasts, nourishes the hunter. It is there that he has the sum of relationships that make him what he is. . . . It is precisely because the jungle is there and is terrible and dangerous that the Negro writer writes and lives at all.[26]

Redding's assertion about the element of necessity, of struggle as playing a significant role in the accomplishments of Black poets and writers, may be at once more specifically and more generally applied. It must have been the jungle, the entangling and seemingly insurmountable odds, that made Redding himself hunt, conquer, gain recognition as a scholar. Yet we must be amazed, given the odds, at the magnitude of his accomplishment: Phi Beta Kappa; author of a prodigious number of books, articles, and reviews ranging the gamut of autobiography, fiction, critical analysis, historical account, and social commentary; winner of the Mayflower award for distinguished writing; recipient of numerous fellowships, including the Guggenheim, the Rockefeller, and the Ford, and of several citations for distinguished achievement; exchange lecturer in foreign countries; researcher on American life and collector of southern folk material; member of the fiction award committee of the National Book Award and of the editorial board of the *American Scholar*. It is not from the standpoint of the scholar Redding, who can explain enigma, then, but from that of the baffled poet that we offer an utterance about Jay Saunders Redding: "Yet do we marvel at this curious thing: to make a scholar black, and bid him redeem."

Notes

1. *No Day of Triumph* (New York: Harper, 1942), p. 4.
2. Ibid., p. 5.
3. Ibid., p. 6.
4. Ibid., p. 9.
5. Ibid., pp. 9– 10.
6. Ibid., p. 10.
7. Ibid., pp. 30– 31, 33.
8. *On Being Negro in America* (Indianapolis: Bobbs-Merrill, 1951), p. 43.
9. *No Day of Triumph*, pp. 35– 36.
10. Ibid., p. 37.
11. Ibid., p. 39.
12. *On Being Negro in America*, pp. 12– 15.
13. Ibid., p. 15.
14. Ibid., p. 26.
15. *An American in India: A Personal Report on the Indian Dilemma and the Nature of Her Conflicts* (Indianapolis: Bobbs-Merrill, 1954), p. 11.
16. Ibid., pp. 139– 46.
17. Ibid., pp. 146– 47.
18. See ibid., pp. 17– 19, 48, 67– 68, 114– 15, 128– 29, 137.
19. Speech to the Contemporary Club, Mar. 19, 1956; Commencement Address at Crispus Attucks High School, Indianapolis, June 10, 1959; and Address to Alpha Boulé, Apr. 7, 1963, Philadelphia, Jay Saunders Redding— Speeches and Reports File, Archives, Hampton Institute, Hampton, Va.
20. Talk at Phyllis Wheatley YWCA, Nov. 1950, ibid.
21. *The Lonesome Road: The Story of the Negro's Part in America* (New York: Doubleday and Co., 1958)

22. Hollie I. West, "Saunders Redding on What It Means to Be Black," *Washington Post,* Jan. 31, 1971, sec. K. p. 1, col. 4, and p. 4, col. 1.

23. Interview with Jay Saunders Redding, professor emeritus at Cornell University, Hampton Institute, Hampton, Va., Aug. 21, 1975.

24. "Yet Do I Marvel," *Color* (New York: Harper, 1925), p. 3.

25. *To Make a Poet Black* (Chapel Hill: Univ. North Carolina Press, 1939), p. vii.

26. "The Negro Writer and His Relationship to His Roots," Conference of Negro Writers, New York, N.Y., 1960, Speeches and Reports File.

Bibliography
Contributors

Bibliography

The sources described below are located in the archives of Hampton Institute, Hampton, Virginia.

Annual Reports of the Principal [President], 1868—;

These printed reports submitted yearly to the Board of Trustees highlight the various activities undertaken by each department of the school and publish a general financial statement. In addition, and of great interest, they reflect the philosophies and cultural attitudes of educators prominent in the development of Black institutions and help explain the directions such education took.

Annual Reports of the Treasurer, 1868—.

These printed reports include tables of receipts and expenditures and an individual list of each bequest to the school during the respective academic year. Thus, they present a detailed picture of the financial health of the school, suggest the extent of its domestic and foreign contacts, and reflect its educational priorities.

Armstrong, Samuel Chapman. *Annual Report to the Commissioner of Indian Affairs*. Washington, D.C.: Government Printing Office, 1882–83, 1885.

Of those submitted annually from 1879 to 1912 by the principal of Hampton Institute, these three reports alone are extant in Hampton's archives. They contain detailed accounts of educational programs for the Indians, findings of follow-up studies made of Indian students who returned to their tribes, appeals for increased federal support, and position statements and recommendations that frequently influenced national Indian policy.

Hollis Burke Frissell Papers.

In addition to other documents and memorabilia, this collection contains all of Frissell's outgoing correspondence from March 1894 through October 25, 1917, a total of more than ninety thousand letters, including letters to such notables as Paul Laurence Dunbar and William Howard Taft.

James Abram Garfield Papers.

This file contains letters from Garfield to Samuel Chapman Armstrong, copies of speeches made at Hampton Institute, newspaper clippings, and photographs.

The *Hampton Student*, March 15, 1909, to December 15, 1924.

This semimonthly journal printed a few editorials about current issues but concentrated on describing notable visitors to the campus, extracurricular activities of the students, and trips taken by the staff.

John, Walton C. *Hampton Normal and Agricultural Institute: Its Evolution and Contribution to Education as a Land Grant College.* Prepared for Bureau of Education, U.S. Department of Interior, Bulletin no. 27. Washington, D.C.: Government Printing Office, 1923.

As the letter of transmittal states, this study was undertaken to describe the fruits of a deeply considered, financially sound system of education in farming, mechanics, home economics, and teacher education.

Kiquotan Kamera Klub Papers.

This material contains club minutes, treasurers' reports, correspondence, photographs of the members, and examples of their work including loose photos and bound projects, among which are found the dummies to the illustrated editions of Paul Laurence Dunbar's *Poems of Cabin and Field* and *Candle-Lightin' Time,* published in cooperation with Dodd, Mead and Company.

Ludlow, Helen W. *Ten Years Work for the Indians.* Hampton: Hampton Institute Press, 1888.

This compilation details the development of an education plan for Indians and its results based on graduates and former students who returned to their tribes.

Massenburg Law File; Race Separation File.

These two folders contain local newspaper clippings, letters to and from Principal James E. Gregg and members of the Board of Trustees and influential public figures, and notes on Gregg's meeting with Governor Byrd of Virginia, 1925–26.

Minutes of the Board of Trustees, 1870—.

These bound volumes, kept in the office of the president of Hampton Institute, contain very detailed records of all regular meetings of the Board of Trustees and the Executive Committee and show, for example, William Howard Taft's personal involvement in the school's fund-raising efforts as well as in its controversies with the federal government over certain properties and his response to the Massenburg Law.

Jay Saunders Redding—Speeches and Reports File and Book Reviews File.

The former collection contains several reports and approximately fifty speeches submitted and delivered primarily during 1955–65. The latter contains over 350 book reviews submitted for publication during the period from 1949 to 1959. The reviews cover autobiography, fiction, critical analyses, historical accounts, and social commentaries.

William H. Sheppard Papers.

This accumulation contains all of Sheppard's known published writings, a corrected MS copy of "Sheppard on Africa," MS copies of addresses, photographs, correspondence, and newspaper and magazine clippings that either mention Sheppard directly or relate to missionary activity in the Congo.

The *Southern Workman,* January 1872 to July 1939.

The *Southern Workman* was the official monthly journal of the college. It printed columns on campus events and on the activities of Black and Indian graduates, articles on Black American organizations, missionaries in Africa, agricultural and industrial developments, book reviews, and obituaries. It contains reports and editorials on a wide range of subjects and materials relating to William Howard Taft, Paul Laurence Dunbar, William H. Sheppard, and Hampton's Indian students—prominent associates of Hampton Institute mentioned in this volume of archival publications. The *Southern Workman* is an invaluable resource not only for the perspective it offers on sixty-seven years of southern life and education, but also because it contains primary documents such as the printed texts of addresses by President Taft, Dr. Sheppard, and Booker T. Washington.

William Howard Taft Papers.

This file contains correspondence between Taft and Hollis Burke Frissell and between Taft and James E. Gregg, speeches delivered at, and speeches delivered on behalf of, Hampton Institute, newspaper clippings, photographs, and memorabilia such as invitations to testimonial dinners.

22 Years' Work of Hampton Normal and Agricultural Institute. Hampton: Hampton Institute Press, 1893.

This anonymous compilation, the preface of which was initialed by Helen W. Ludlow, describes the school's program for Blacks and Indians, giving special attention to the records of its graduates and former students.

Contributors

FRANCES A. GRIMES is Professor of English and chairman of the Department of English at Hampton Institute. A graduate of Tuskegee Institute, she holds the M.A. from Southern Illinois University and the Ph.D. from The Ohio State University, where she studied under a fellowship from the Ford Foundation. She has edited several publications and developed and coordinated projects for public presentation. An active member of several professional organizations, a public speaker, and a contributor to the 1977 supplement to *American Notes and Queries (First Person Female)*, she is at present preparing articles on Chaucer, Stephen Crane, and Ernest Gaines.

NANCY B. MCGHEE, Avalon Professor of the Humanities, earned her A.B. from Shaw University, her M.A. from Columbia University, and her Ph.D. from the University of Chicago, concentrating her doctoral research on the Negro preacher in American literature before 1900. She has done further study at the University of London and at Cambridge University. Recipient of Hampton Institute's distinguished teaching award, member and officer of many professional organizations, Dr. McGhee has published numerous articles, including the recent paper "Langston Hughes: Poet in the Folk Manner."

WILLIAM H. ROBINSON, Professor of Education, joined Hampton Institute in 1946 after taking his B.S. at Virginia State College and his M.A. at Hampton. Studying under a Ford Foundation Fellowship, he completed his Ph.D. in the history and philosophy of education at New York University in 1954. He has done postdoctoral work at Harvard University. Dr. Robinson has served as founder and director of Hampton Institute's educational program on the Virgin Islands, chairman of the Department of Secondary Education, director of the Division of Education, and dean of the Graduate Division. His most recent publication is "Desegregation and Higher Education," published in *School and Society*.

LARRYETTA M. SCHALL, Associate Professor of English, holds degrees from the University of Pennsylvania and the University of Nevada

(Reno), where she did her doctoral research on proletarian protest ballads during the English Rennaissance, an interest she is currently pursuing in several related areas. Dr. Schall is director of the Freshman Interdisciplinary Program, an experimental course which combines classes in history, reading, speech, and English. An active member of many civic and professional organizations, she has recently delivered papers on the ballads of Bob Dylan and Thomas Deloney and on Shakespeare's *Coriolanus* to the Popular Culture Association.

CHARLES D. WALTERS, Professor of Graduate Education, came to Hampton Institute in 1970. He received his B.S. and M.Ed. from the University of South Carolina and his Ed.D. from The George Washington University. Dr. Walters has served as chairman of the Secondary Education Department and has held offices in numerous community organizations. He has published widely both as a poet and as a scholar, his most recent contributions being a paper on educational technology in *American Educational Research Association Bulletin* and a poem entitled "Peach Child" in the *Anthology of College Poetry*.

HOWARD V. YOUNG, JR., is a native of Branford, Connecticut, where he attended the public schools. He was a student at Southern Connecticut State College in New Haven until he joined the U.S. Air Force in 1943. After returning from England, where he was stationed until 1945, he completed his A.B. from Middlebury College and his M.A. and Ph.D. from Brown University. Dr. Young has been on the Hampton Institute faculty since 1951 and has served for a decade as chairman of the History Department. Currently, he is coordinator of the Eastern Virginia International Studies Consortium involving five colleges and universities in the Tidewater area.